Life is not boring to one who believes in adventure. Adventure does not mean that you have to climb up the tallest mountain. To allow new ideas, fresh ideas, healthy ideas to enter into your mind — that is adventure.

SRI CHINMOY

On Yoga, meditation, and the art of living

The Adventure of Life

Sri Chinmoy

ISBN 978-3-89532-294-5

The Golden Shore Verlagsges.mbH
Austraße 76 · 90429 Nürnberg · Germany
www.goldenshore.de

www.bluebeyondbooks.co.uk

Printed in the Czech Republic.

CONTENTS

Freedom and peace · 8

What is Yoga? · 12

Yoga and the material life · 16

The path and steps of Yoga · 24

Religion, spirituality and Yoga · 28

God and the higher worlds · 38

Kundalini Yoga, the chakras and occult power · 54

True and false Masters · 60

Spirituality and society · 66

The end of the world, evil forces, and the origin
of mankind · 78

Meditation · 84

Food, health and fitness · 106

Family life · 116

Meditation in the workplace · 126

EDITORIAL NOTE

Sri Chinmoy's words presented here have been selected from his writings, lectures and answers to questions, which he offered to spiritual seekers, university students and luminaries from all walks of life over the years. In the process of compiling this book — which included excerpting text from longer passages, transcribing recordings of Sri Chinmoy's voice and highlighting parts we found especially inspiring — we have strived to stay true to the original context and convey Sri Chinmoy's philosophy as he expressed it during his life. However, may we suggest to the interested reader to explore the original, unabbreviated versions of the texts, which can be found at *www.srichinmoylibrary.com.*

PREFACE

Life is adventure.

Whether learning to walk, playing the flute, writing a novel, climbing a mountain or practising meditation, the adventure of life is an exploration of the limits of our capacities, and the quest to transcend them.

We are not merely our physical bodies, life energy, rational minds and passing emotions. The vaster realm of our self is the spiritual, which infuses, inspires and fulfils our outer life. To discover, explore and grow into the spiritual wealth of our limitless soul is the crowning purpose of our life, its ultimate adventure.

Yet how to connect this lofty purpose with our present world, so fraught with confusion, anxiety and stress? Here the all-encompassing wisdom of a spiritual Master can shed light and offer hope, comfort and guidance.

With selections from the writings of Sri Chinmoy on numerous aspects of our everyday life, this volume is a treasure house of inspiration for the journey.

— *editors*

CHAPTER ONE

Freedom and peace

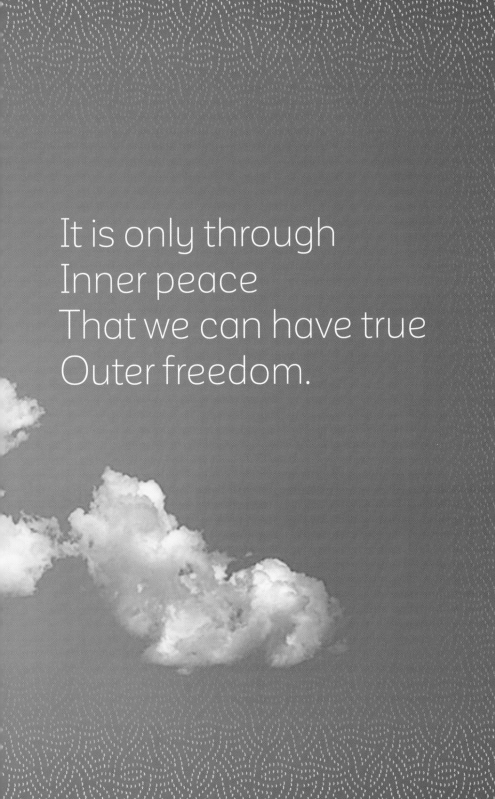

It is only through
Inner peace
That we can have true
Outer freedom.

The source of freedom

Freedom is happiness. Freedom is fullness. Freedom can be otherwise, as well. Freedom can bring about untold miseries. Human beings need freedom — freedom from tyranny, freedom from slavery, freedom from bondage, freedom from ignorance. Some human beings want freedom in creation, while others want freedom in destruction. Still others need freedom in aspiration and dedication.

We fight for the outer freedom. We cry for the inner freedom. With the outer freedom, we see and rule the four corners of the globe. With the inner freedom, we see the Soul and become the Goal of the entire universe.

> I feel that freedom lives in peace and nowhere else.
>
> If you have inner peace, nobody can force you to be a slave to the outer reality.

No price is too great to pay for inner peace. Peace is the harmonious control of life. It is vibrant with life-energy. It is a power that easily transcends all our worldly knowledge. Yet it is not separate from our earthly existence. If we open the right avenues within, this peace can be felt here and now.

The greatest misfortune that can come to a human being is to lose his inner peace. No outer force can rob him of it. It is his own thoughts, his own actions that rob him of it.

The whole world is captured by restlessness and nervousness. The very aim of practising Yoga is to have peace, peace of mind. When one acquires peace of mind, automatically one possesses indomitable inner strength. How can nervousness enter into a person when he is surcharged with inner strength? There can be no restlessness, no nervousness. Nervousness comes when you take away a part from the whole. Fear comes when you separate something from the whole.

We must not allow our past to torment and destroy the peace of our heart. Our present good and divine actions can easily counteract our bad and undivine actions of the past. If sin has the power to make us weep, meditation has undoubtedly the power to give us joy, to endow us with the divine wisdom.

Our peace is within, and this peace is the basis of our life.

Our peace is within, and this peace is the basis of our life. So from today let us resolve to fill our minds and hearts with the tears of devotion, the foundation of peace. If our foundation is solid, then no matter how high we raise the superstructure, danger can never threaten us. For peace is below, peace is above, peace is within, peace is without.

CHAPTER TWO

What is Yoga?

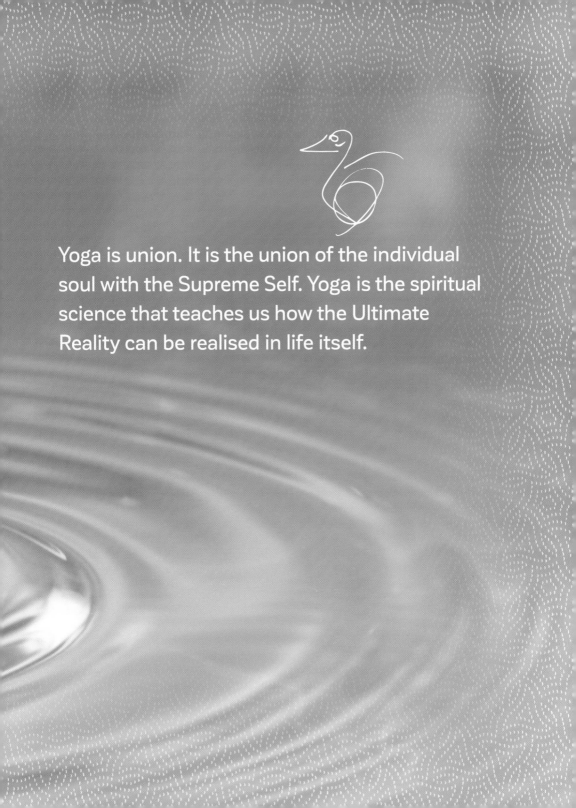

Yoga is union. It is the union of the individual soul with the Supreme Self. Yoga is the spiritual science that teaches us how the Ultimate Reality can be realised in life itself.

Yoga and life

Without Yoga there is no self-discovery. Yoga is not a religion. Yoga is the Universal Truth. It is the traditional truth of India. It is the most important experience of life. True Yoga and life go together. They cannot be separated. If you try to separate them, you will fail. Yoga and life are as inseparable as the Creator and the creation.

Anybody can practice Yoga and it can be practiced irrespective of age. But we must understand what Yoga really involves. Unfortunately, there are many people who think that Yoga means physical postures and breathing exercises. This is a deplorable mistake. These postures and exercises are preliminary and preparatory states, leading towards concentration and meditation, which alone can take us to deeper, higher and fuller life.

Hatha Yoga is the starting point. Practising Hatha Yoga is like studying in kindergarten, whereas concentration, meditation and contemplation are the university courses. Even if you do not study in the kindergarten, you may easily get to the university. There are some good students, brilliant students, who skip some grades. They need not go to kindergarten. They start in primary school and then continue. But if you don't start, then how are you going to reach your destination? Whatever Hatha Yoga can teach us, we should willingly learn, but we must not give undue importance to this small branch of the great tree of Yoga.

If your body is not strong enough, then today you will suffer from a stomach-ache, tomorrow you will have a headache and the next day you will have some other disorder. Naturally, you will not be able to concentrate and meditate. For that reason it is important to keep the body fit. And Hatha Yoga *asanas* are far better for the body than the vigorous exercises that are done in the West. *Asanas* will soothe your body as long as you do not do them too much. If *asanas* are done too dynamically, they may arouse aggressive feelings. But when you do them correctly, you get a kind, mild, soft vibration.

Hatha Yoga may help us a little bit spiritually, but we have to know where we stand in our spiritual journey. If we are very restless, we can do Hatha Yoga in the beginning to learn to sit calmly and quietly. But if we are not constant victims of restlessness, even if we are absolute beginners, Hatha Yoga is not needed, for when we enter into meditation we automatically enter into a calm, quiet state. By doing Hatha Yoga exercises, we feel that we are regulating and disciplining our life. But when we meditate properly and life-energy enters into us from our meditation, automatically our life is disciplined. The divine Peace and Light which we need, we can never, never get from Hatha Yoga. So if you want to do *asanas* for five or ten minutes daily to keep your body fit, you can do so. But if you want to do Hatha Yoga for two hours before you meditate, it will be a sheer waste of time.

What is Yoga? Yoga is self-conquest. Self-conquest is God-realisation. He who practises Yoga does two things with one stroke: he simplifies his whole life and he gets a free access to the Divine.

In the field of Yoga we can never pretend. Our aspiration must ring true. Our whole life must ring true. Nothing is impossible for an ardent aspirant. A higher Power guides his steps. God's adamantine Will is his safest protection. No matter how long or how many times he blunders, he has every right to come back to his own spiritual home. His aspiration is a climbing flame. It has no smoke, it needs no fuel. It is the breath of his inner life. It leads him to the shores of the Golden Beyond. The aspirant, with the wings of his aspiration, soars into the realms of the Transcendental.

Yoga means union. Union with whom? It is the union with God. By practising Yoga, that is, spiritual discipline, we unite ourselves with God.

CHAPTER THREE

Yoga and the material life

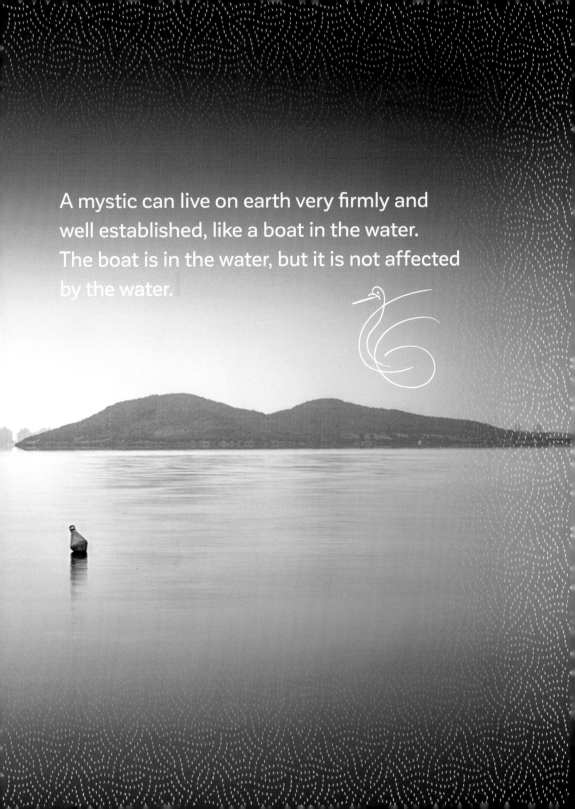

A mystic can live on earth very firmly and well established, like a boat in the water. The boat is in the water, but it is not affected by the water.

The infinite treasure

Yoga helps us in our everyday life. As a matter of fact, it is Yoga that can serve as the supreme help in our daily lives. Our human life is full of doubt, fear and frustration. Yoga helps us to replace fear with indomitable courage, doubt with absolute certainty, and frustration with golden achievement.

Question: What response would you give to a person who asks, "How does the spiritual life benefit the man on the street, the man who is more concerned about getting bread and maintaining his life?"

Sri Chinmoy: If he is more concerned about earning his bread, that means that he needs money-power. If he has money, then he can buy bread. Now, we have to know what helps us in getting money. It is energy, labour, strength and effort. All these things come from within. If a person follows the spiritual life, he will be surcharged with energy. The spiritual life can inspire people in any sphere of life; it can help anybody on earth. Spirituality, in the strict sense of the term, is for God-realisation. But if one does not want to go so far, if one only wants to make some progress in the material life in order to become prosperous, he can use prayer. Prayer is a form of spirituality; meditation is a form of spirituality. His prayer and meditation will help him to make more money and become more prosperous. But that is not the real aim of the spiritual life. The aim of the spiritual life is to get the infinite treasure, the infinite Light of the Supreme, which is always for us to use. But if worldly people practise meditation and prayer, the things that they want will not be taken away. On the contrary, they will get them in abundant measure.

Question: Can I strive for material wealth in my outer life and still be at peace in my inner life?

Sri Chinmoy: Certainly, but we have to know how much material wealth we require. It has to be in proportion to our need. If we want to become the richest person on earth, for that also we can pray and meditate. But we have to know where this prayer is leading us. If we become the richest man by virtue of our prayer, will we be happy? Our prayer and meditation tell us only one thing: God is all Joy. If we pray to God to make us the richest person on earth, God may listen to our prayer, but

> *If we become the richest man by virtue of our prayer, will we be happy?*

happiness is something totally different. In this world, when God gives us material power, we see that this money-power is not what we really need. Love-power, oneness-power, is what we need.

We may be a millionaire, a billionaire, but when we see that people do not love us, our hearts will break. Like beggars, we will cry for love from others. But our material power, our money-power, is not going to win their love. Only our love-power, our oneness-power, is going to win their love. So when we pray to God, we should ask only for one thing: "Let Thy Will be done." If it is God's Will to make an individual the richest person, then God will do it. But if God's Will is something different, then God will act in a different way. We can pray to God for material power, but we have to be sincere to our cause. Do we want real happiness in life? If we want real happiness in life, then we have to know that material power can be an obstacle to our God-discovery.

Question: I would frankly like to know what India's spirituality has ever done for her. How is it that in spite of her yogis and saints, she is still a poor and backward country?

Sri Chinmoy: First, we must understand what has brought this situation about. In ancient India, the material life was not renounced. People in those days aspired for a synthesis of Matter and Spirit, and to some extent they were successful in achieving it. But there is a great gulf between that hoary past and the present.

In the later periods of India's history, the saints and seers came to feel that the material life and the spiritual life could never go together, that they had to renounce the outer life in order to attain to God. Hence, the external life was neglected. This led to foreign conquests and many other troubles. Even today, the attitude that material prosperity and beauty should be negated is very common in India. This accounts for much of her continued poverty.

But at present there are spiritual giants in India who feel that God should be realised in His totality, that Creator and creation are one and inseparable. They advocate the acceptance of life, the real need for both progress and perfection in all spheres of human existence. This new approach is widely accepted in modern India.

India may be poverty-stricken today, but she will progress quickly by virtue of her new awareness and her new aspiration. She has not only magnanimity of heart but also the power to bring her soul's strength to the fore and use it to solve all her problems.

Question: Many people get up in the morning, swallow a quick breakfast, run out of the house and go to the subway, get to work and get completely involved with everyday survival. And before the end of the day it's pretty tough to sit back and take a spiritual view of what's going on because you have to go out there and hustle. You have to earn a living. Is there a way of integrating the spiritual life into what we call the economic life?

Sri Chinmoy: Our philosophy is the philosophy of wisdom: first things first. Most human beings are wanting in peace, peace of mind. They enter into the hustle and bustle of life right in the morning, and during the whole day they do not have even an iota of peace. We feel that if we can do first things first we are being wise. Early in the morning, if we can pray to God for at least a few minutes, that means we are doing first things first.

We feel it is money-power, material wealth that will give us satisfaction. But it is not material power; it is the inner power, spiritual power that gives us real satisfaction. If God the Almighty Father is satisfied with us, if He is pleased with us, then He will grant us peace of mind. And once we have peace of mind, no matter where we go and what activities we enter into, still we feel a sense of satisfaction. Right now satisfaction is a far cry. But early in the morning if we pray to God and meditate on God for a few minutes, then we get peace of mind to some extent. And this peace of mind is undoubtedly true satisfaction in life.

The journey from desire to aspiration

We often feel in our daily experience that desire is one thing and God is something else. Desire, we say, is bad in the spiritual life, for when we desire something, we feel it is the object itself that we desire. It is true that through aspiration alone we can realise God, but we have to know that God abides in our desire as well as in our aspiration. When we come to realise that desire also has its existence in God, we get our first illumination.

Our earthly journey starts with desire, and in the ordinary life we cannot live without it. But if we feel that we are not ready for the spiritual life just because we have teeming desires, then I wish to say we will never be ready for the spiritual life. We have to start our spiritual journey here and now, even while we are walking along the path of desire.

Let us take desire as an object and try to feel the Breath of God inside it. Slowly and unmistakably the Breath of God will come to the fore and transform our desire into aspiration. Then, if we apply this process to aspiration as well, we will come to feel that our aspiration and our earthly existence can never be separated.

There are two kinds of men on earth who do not have desire: those who have liberated souls and those who have dull, inert, lifeless souls. Liberated souls have freed themselves from bondage, limitations and imperfections. They have become free from ignorance and have become one with their souls in transcendental illumination. Again, some human beings want nothing from life. They just wallow in the pleasures of idleness and lethargy; they have no aspiration for anything. So they will never, never have illumination.

You have to start

The great spiritual hero, Swami Vivekananda, was once asked by a young man how he might realise God. Vivekananda said, "From now on start telling lies." The young man said, "You want me to tell lies? How then can I realise God? It is against spiritual principles." But Vivekananda said, "I know better than you. I know what your standard is. You won't budge an inch; you are useless, you are practically dead to the ordinary life, not to speak of the spiritual life. If you start telling lies, people will pinch you and strike you, and then you will exert your own personality. First you have to develop your own individuality and personality. Then a day will come when you will have to surrender your individuality and personality to the divine Wisdom, the infinite Light and Bliss. But you have to start your journey first."

The middle path without extremes is the best. We have to be normal; we have to be sound in our day-to-day life.

There are some unbalanced persons who feel that they will realise God by walking along the street like a vagabond or by torturing their body and remaining weak. Their physical weakness they take as a harbinger of God-realisation. The great Lord Buddha tried the path of self-mortification, but he came to the conclusion that the middle path without extremes is the best. We have to be normal; we have to be sound in our day-to-day life. Aspiration is not one thing and our physical body something else. No! Our heart's aspiration and our physical body go together; the physical aspiration and the psychic aspiration can and must run together.

Desire means anxiety. This anxiety finds satisfaction only when it is able to fulfil itself through solid attachment. Aspiration means calmness. This calmness finds satisfaction only when it is able to express itself through all-seeing and all-loving detachment.

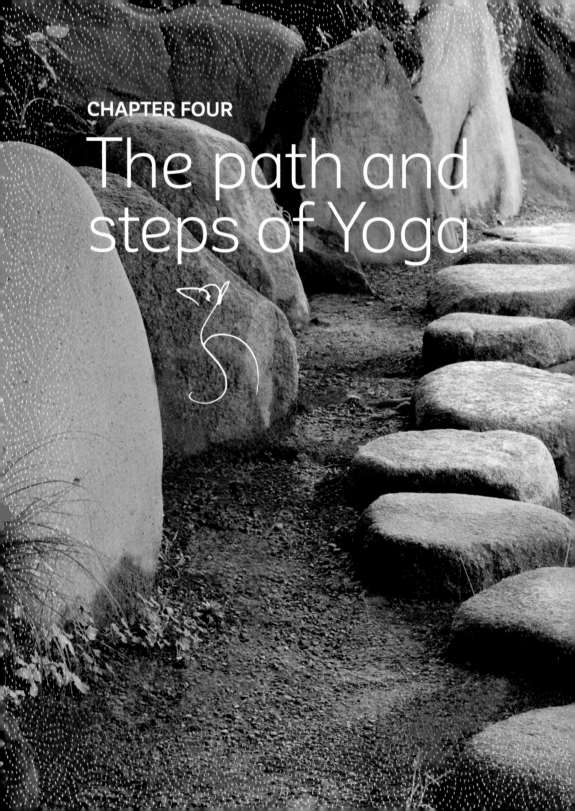

CHAPTER FOUR
The path and steps of Yoga

We are one with the Spirit, but right now we are not aware of it. We can be aware of it only when we consciously practise spirituality, and for that we need aspiration. When we desire, we bind ourselves; when we aspire, we free ourselves.

Set on the journey

According to our traditional Hindu system, there are three major yogas — Karma Yoga, Bhakti Yoga and Jnana Yoga. Karma Yoga is the yoga of dedicated service. Bhakti Yoga is the yoga of love and devotion. Jnana Yoga is the yoga of knowledge and wisdom. In Jnana Yoga we see an important, most powerful branch called Raja Yoga. In the West, this is what you call mysticism, yoga for the mystics.

There are eight steps in the spiritual *sadhana* or discipline: *Yama, Niyama, Asana, Pranayama, Pratyahara, Dharana, Dhyana* and *Samadhi. Yama* is self-control and moral abstinence; *Niyama* is strict observance of conduct and character; *Asana* is body posture meant to help calm the body and make it a receptive instrument; *Pranayama* is systematic breathing to calm and help control the mind; *Pratyahara* is withdrawal from the sense-life; *Dharana* is fixation of the consciousness on God; *Dhyana* is meditation; and *Samadhi* is trance, the absolute union of the individual consciousness with the universal Consciousness.

We do not have to go through all the preliminary stages once we begin to aspire consciously. We do not have to go through the Hatha Yoga asanas and Pranayama in order to enter into meditation. Self-control, withdrawal from the sense-life and fixation of the consciousness on God are necessary to some extent before true aspiration can begin. But once aspiration enters into our unillumined human life, our journey has begun.

If we have aspiration, we can start with concentration, meditation and contemplation.

You do not have to go deliberately through *Yama, Niyama, Asana* and *Pranayama.* If you really enter into the field of aspiration, immediately you will try to give up wrong things. You will automatically lead a moral and controlled life. You will stop doing things that are detrimental to your spiritual life. Your inner cry, your aspiration, will compel you to practise the first two steps. And you will find that the third and fourth stages are not necessary.

The sunlit path

As they say, slow and steady wins the race, and you can go step by step, slowly and steadily. But there is also a path called the sunlit path. All roads lead to the same Goal, but there is one particular road which will lead you there sooner than the other roads. That road is the path of concentration, deep meditation and one-pointed contemplation. One can certainly practise *Pratyahara* without first practising the other disciplines. And if one also wants to skip *Pratyahara* and start with *Dharana* or *Dhyana*, one can also do that. Many spiritual seekers have done it, and they have been successful in their spiritual journey. But it is up to the individual whether or not he feels the need for any of the particular steps.

I have told my disciples that it is not at all necessary to begin before *Dhyana*. They meditate with me, and they have high, sublime experiences without all the preceding disciplines. But there are other spiritual Masters who ask their students to go through other stages. I have nothing to say against that. Each one has his own way of realising the Truth and offering the Truth to others. If you are sincere enough to follow a spiritual path to the end, and if you have a spiritual Master or if you have friends who are far advanced in the spiritual life, then you can take their help and suggestions on how to make the fastest progress.

> What is aspiration? Aspiration is man's conscious cry to climb up to the Highest, to run the Farthest and dive the Deepest.

CHAPTER FIVE
Religion, spirituality and Yoga

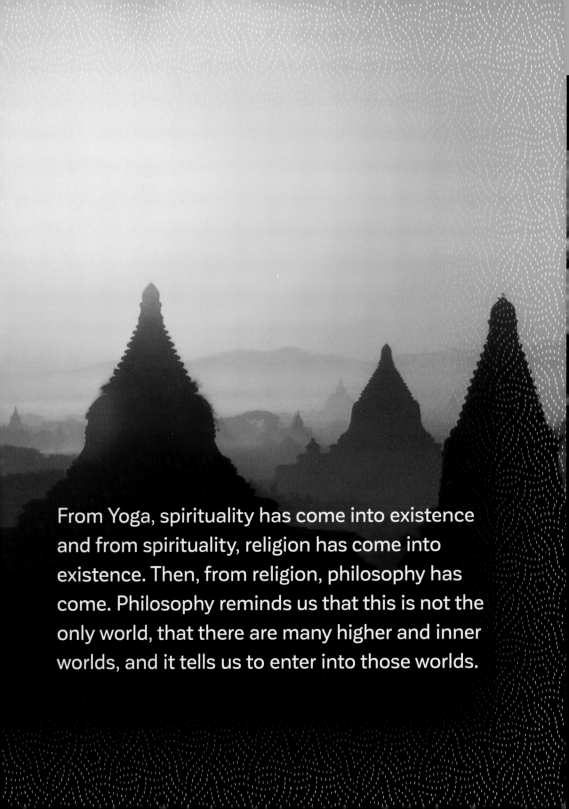

From Yoga, spirituality has come into existence and from spirituality, religion has come into existence. Then, from religion, philosophy has come. Philosophy reminds us that this is not the only world, that there are many higher and inner worlds, and it tells us to enter into those worlds.

Feeling of oneness-heart

The essence of every religion is love of God. There is not a single religion that does not tell us to love God. The problem comes with the followers of religion. Very often they say, "My religion is by far the best, whereas your religion is very bad." The followers of the different religions are like children in a family. The children have the same parents and receive the same affection, love and compassion from their parents. But still the children quarrel and fight. If one sister sees that another sister is more beautiful, then immediately she becomes jealous and quarrels with the other one. If one brother sees that another brother is more powerful, immediately the weak one speaks ill of the strong one. Again, in a family, many times one brother will say, "I know better than anybody!" and the other brother will say, "No, I know better than you!" Similarly, each religion will tell its brother and sister religions, "I know more about the Heavenly Father than you do." Or they will say, "My way of loving God is the only correct way, and your way is wrong." So, quite often it happens that there is quarrelling and fighting among the various religions.

But one thing all religions agree on is love of God. And if we really love someone, we feel our oneness with that person. So if we really love God and feel our oneness with God, we will also feel our oneness with God's creation. In the inmost depths of our heart we know that we are all one, but then pride enters into us and we tell others, "I do not need you." But we *do* need one another. We are all part and parcel of the same existence-reality. A tree consists of the trunk, branches, leaves, flowers and fruits. If the trunk says that it does not need the branches or leaves, then what kind of tree will it be? And if the flowers say that they do not need the branches and trunk, then how will they live? So unity has to be established.

When we enter into a garden, immediately we become aware of the beauty, purity and fragrance of the garden. Each flower has its own beauty, but the beauty we feel in the garden is the beauty of multiplicity. And this is the beauty that gives us immense joy. Similarly, God gets immense Joy from the multiplicity of the flower-hearts of all His children.

In religion, the feeling of oneness-heart has to prevail, and nothing else. Religion is not a matter of reason. If we live in our oneness-heart, we will feel the essence of all religions, which is love of God. But if we live in the mind, we will only try to separate one religion from another and see how their ideologies differ. It is the heart that can have a true intuitive understanding of the height and breadth of all religions. It is the heart that sees and feels the inner harmony and oneness of all religions.

True religion has a universal quality. It does not find fault with other religions. False religions will find fault with other religions; they will say that theirs is the only valid religion and their prophet

Religion and philosophy fulfil and are complementary to each other. Religion without philosophy is brainless. Philosophy without religion is heartless.

is the only saviour. But a true religion will feel that all the prophets are saviours of mankind. Forgiveness, compassion, tolerance, brotherhood and the feeling of oneness are the signs of a true religion.

Question: Do you think that all religions lead to the same truth, but maybe by different routes?

Sri Chinmoy: I do, absolutely. I fully agree that all religions lead to one truth, the Absolute Truth. There is one Truth. There is only one Goal, but there are various paths. Each religion is right in its own way. But, if one religion says that it is the only religion, or by far the best, at that point I find it difficult to see eye to eye with that particular religion. If a religion says, "My religion is true. Your religion is equally true," then I wholeheartedly agree. But, if I say that our Hinduism is by far the best and that your Christianity is nowhere near Hinduism, then I am the worst possible fool on earth. If I say, "If you accept my religion, then I will take you to the Goal sooner," and if I try to convert you to my religion, then again I am committing a Himalayan blunder.

No. Each religion is right. A religion is a house. I have to live in my house. You have to live in your house. I cannot stay in the street; you cannot either. But a day comes when we widen our vision. We feel that beyond the boundary of the rites and rituals of religion lies a higher Goal. Then what can we do? We can try to perfect the imperfection in the religion. Then immediately we will come into conflict with the fanatics. Or we find that we are not in a position to change the rules and canons of the religion. Then we are miserable. But, if we follow the spiritual life, the inner life, we are not in conflict with any religion. So we say that those who want to follow a religion should follow it. But those who want to follow a still higher Goal, that is to say Yoga, the conscious and constant union with God, must follow the path of Yoga. There, on the strength of our oneness with God, we say that the entire world is ours. Each human being is our brother, our sister. When you launch into the field of Yoga and want to realise the highest Truth, absolutely the highest Truth, at that time I wish to tell you that you can be above your religion. That is to say, if you don't want to follow your religion or any religion, you are free to do it because you are crying for the Highest in a special way. Your religion and my religion, in spite of their respective imperfections, are aiming at the same Goal. But now you may feel that you have a tremendous inner urge to reach the Highest without involving yourself in the so-called limitations of your religion, my religion and other religions. Then naturally you will try to reach your Goal without disturbing us, without disturbing others, and at the same time you yourself will not be disturbed.

The highest type of spirituality Does not need rituals at all.

Listen to the soul

The spiritual life is the life of the soul. We have to become consciously one with our soul. It is only when we feel our oneness with the soul that true satisfaction can dawn in our lives. We can never be truly satisfied with our own outer satisfaction. We can only be permanently happy when we satisfy God in God's own Way. God is our highest Reality. The more we listen to the soul within us, the more we grow into the highest Reality within us, and only then can we be eternally satisfied.

Question: There is disharmony between my parents and myself because my father is an atheist.

Sri Chinmoy: What is wrong with being an atheist? You believe in God's Love and he believes in something else. There is nobody on earth who does not believe in something. He will believe in his food, or in his body, or in a flower or in football or in science. He has to believe in something that he has seen or he has to believe in nothing. So tell your father, "You are an atheist, but you believe in something."

You believe in God; your father believes in something else. Even nothing is a reality. Our Indian philosophy says, *Neti, neti* — "Not this, not that." This nothing also comes from the mind and heart. You can tell your father to have faith in that nothing, and he will see your God in this nothing. You can say, "I say 'everything'.

If you want me to define spirituality, I can define it by using only one word: satisfaction. Spirituality is nothing more and nothing less than satisfaction.

You stick to your nothing. Eventually you will see that inside my everything is your nothing, and inside your nothing is my everything."

It is inside the finite that God is manifesting His Infinity. Right now an iota of light is everything to us. But when we go high, even Infinity is nothing because God has given us infinite hunger. We are talking about the supreme realisation. Today your father does not understand what we are talking about, but one day he will understand because he is going to realise this very thing himself.

So do not worry about your father. Tell him only to have faith in what he believes and in what he has. If he sticks to his faith, his problems will be solved. Just encourage him to derive satisfaction from what he believes is true in his life. If he is not satisfied, you can say to him, "You are not getting satisfaction from your beliefs, but I am getting satisfaction from mine, so how can you say that I am wrong? Why don't you try my path?"

> *The difference between the heart and the mind is this: the heart wants to give, the mind hates to lose.*

Question: Can a husband and wife have different teachers?

Sri Chinmoy: If the husband and wife have different teachers, it is like going to the same goal along two roads. Problems will arise if the husband says that his road is clear, sunlit, whereas the wife's road is full of obstacles. Then trouble will start. But if the husband says, "I like this road and you like that road. So you go your own way, I will go my way, and we will reach the same destination," then it is all right. If the husband does not try to convert the wife and the wife does not try to convert the husband, that is the right thing. But when a feeling of comparison or competition enters, then all is lost.

Question: But does the union of two people diminish at all when they are following two different paths to the same thing?

Sri Chinmoy: No. The only thing we have to know is how much understanding and respect they have for each other's path. But it is always safe if they have the same Master, if they are walking along the same road. If the husband and wife follow the same path and the husband becomes tired, exhausted, assailed by doubt, then at that time the wife becomes his helper. And if the wife becomes assailed by doubt or fear, then the husband can be of real help. So if they follow the same path, it is a great advantage.

But if the wife says, "I want to follow the path of the heart," and the husband says, "I want to follow the path of the mind," husband and wife have to be very careful. Each has to know that the other is doing the right thing, according to his or her own capacity and understanding. They should have mutual respect for each other's realisation.

Question: What about the place of women in the spiritual life at this time of 'women's liberation' and all that? What is the woman's real place in a spiritual sense and a man's real place?

Sri Chinmoy: In God's Eye, there is no man, there is no woman. In God's Eye they are one. Man is the face; woman is the smile. Without the face, how can there be a smile? Again, if there is no smile, what good is the face? So both are equally important.

Spirituality is not merely tolerance. It is not even acceptance. It is the feeling of universal oneness. In our spiritual life, we look upon the Divine, not only in terms of our own God, but in terms of everybody's God. Our spiritual life firmly and securely establishes the basis of unity in diversity.

Spirituality is not mere hospitality to others' faith in God. It is the absolute recognition and acceptance of their faith in God as one's own. Difficult, but not impossible, for this has been the experience and practice of all spiritual Masters of all times.

Question: Are you part of a particular organized religious body or a sect or cult, or are you just who you are?

Sri Chinmoy: I belong to no sect and to no religion. At the same time, my teachings embody the quintessence of all religions. I appreciate and admire all religions, but I do not belong to any particular religion. I was born as a Hindu; therefore, I know all the ins and outs of the Hindu religion. But I do not practise Hinduism. I do not follow any specific religion. My religion is to love God and to become a humble instrument of God. The Hindu religion is like a house; Christianity is another house; Judaism is another house. We can each live in a different house, and then come to one school to study. Spirituality, Yoga, is what we eventually must study.

Question: Is there any difference between one religion and another religion? Does Yoga demand renunciation of all religions?

Sri Chinmoy: There is no fundamental difference between one religion and another because each religion embodies the ultimate Truth. So Yoga does not interfere with any religion. Anybody can practise Yoga. I have disciples who are Catholics, Protestants, Jews and so forth. One can practise Yoga irrespective of religion. Now if one has been taught Hinduism, he may be afraid of accepting Catholicism and vice-versa. But the real aspirant who has launched into spirituality and Yoga will find no difficulty in remaining in his own religion. I tell my disciples not to give up their own religion. If they remain in their own religion and practise the spiritual life and the inner discipline, they will go faster because their own religion will give them constant confidence in what they are doing and confirm what they are actually practising in their life. So I always tell my students to stick to their own religion, for Yoga does not demand renunciation of any religion.

We are inside the Heart of God

Religion is no obstacle to the spiritual life. Yoga or spiritual discipline will never find fault with any religion. Yoga means union with God, conscious union with God. I can pray to God in my own way; you pray to God in your own way. God is pleased with both of us. This is religion. Then, when we realise God, we become one with His creation, with His universe. At that time we feel that we are inside the Heart of God. When I realise God, I feel myself inside the Heart of God. You will also do the same.

So we must not criticise any religion. But when it is a matter of Yoga, we have to know that Yoga transcends all religions. Here we don't want to be satisfied only with my house or your house. We want to claim all the houses of the world as our very own because God is inside all of them. In Yoga, all religions become ours, because Yoga means union with God. When we have this union, we transcend our limited feeling of 'my' and 'mine', my religion, your religion. At that time, we go beyond the boundaries of religion.

All religions are true. But when we enter into the spiritual life, we go one step beyond religion. At that time, only God is our aim, our goal.

Religion is the house, spirituality is the living room, Yoga is the prayer and meditation room. The house is beautiful, the living room is meaningful, the prayer and meditation room is fruitful.

If we enter into Him, we enter into the infinite Consciousness. If we pray and we meditate, we accept all religions as our very own and place them in the very Heart of God.

CHAPTER SIX

God and the higher worlds

The purpose of life is to manifest the inner divinity. The purpose of life is to become a conscious instrument, a chosen instrument of God. The purpose of life is to manifest the highest Truth which we embody. First we have to see the Truth and feel the Truth. Then we have to reveal and manifest the Truth.

Finding God

God-realisation, or *siddhi*, means Self-discovery in the highest sense of the term. One consciously realises his oneness with God. As long as the seeker remains in ignorance, he will feel that God is somebody else who has infinite Power, while he, the seeker, is the feeblest person on earth. But the moment he realises God, he comes to know that he and God are absolutely one in both the inner and the outer life. God-realisation means one's identification with one's absolute highest Self. When one can identify with one's highest Self and remain in that consciousness forever, when one can reveal and manifest it at one's own command, that is God-realisation.

Now, you have studied books on God, and people have told you that God is in everybody. But you have not realised God in your conscious life. For you this is all mental speculation. But when one is God-realised, one consciously knows what God is, what He looks like, what He wills. When one achieves Self-realisation, one remains in God's Consciousness and speaks to God face to face. He sees God both in the finite and in the infinite; he sees God as both personal and impersonal. And in his case, this is not mental hallucination or imagination; it is direct reality. This reality is more authentic than my seeing you right here in front of me. When one speaks to a human being, there is always a veil of ignorance: darkness, imperfection, misunderstanding. But between God and the inner being of one who has realised Him, there can be no ignorance, no veil. So at that time one can speak to God more clearly, more convincingly, more openly than to a human being.

As ordinary human beings, we feel that infinite Peace, infinite Light, infinite Bliss and infinite divine Power are all sheer imagination. We are victims to doubt, fear and negative forces which we feel are quite normal and natural. We cannot love anything purely, not even ourselves. We are in the finite, quarrelling and fighting, and there is no such thing as Peace or Light or Bliss in us. But those who practise meditation go deep within and see that there *is* real Peace, Light and Bliss. They get boundless inner strength and see that doubt and fear *can* be challenged and conquered. When we achieve God-realisation, our inner existence is flooded with Peace, Poise, Equanimity and Light.

Illumining our life

In our day-to-day life, we very often speak of bondage and freedom. But realisation says that there is no such thing as bondage and freedom. What actually exists is consciousness — consciousness on various levels, consciousness enjoying itself in its various manifestations. In the field of manifestation, consciousness has different grades. Why do we pray? We pray because our prayer leads us from a lower degree of illumination to a higher degree. We pray because our prayer brings us closer to something pure, beautiful, inspiring and fulfilling. The highest illumination is God-realisation. This illumination must take place not only in the soul, but also in the heart, mind, vital and body. God-realisation is a conscious, complete and perfect union with God.

Question: What is God?

Sri Chinmoy: God is infinite Consciousness, infinite Bliss, yet He can also assume a finite form. He is infinite, He is finite; and at the same time He transcends both the infinite and the finite. He is life, He is death; yet again He is beyond both life and death. When I say 'Supreme', I am referring to the Infinite, the Eternal and the Immortal. But when I see Him, I see Him face to face the same way I see you. But in fact God is boundless and in the field of manifestation He takes all forms, from that of a tiny insect to that of a large elephant. Many people cannot agree with the idea that God can be finite. But let us think of one of God's divine qualities called Omnipresence. According to our human feeling, when we think of omnipresence we immediately think of vastness. True, He is as vast as the world, but because He is in everything, God can also be finite. Again, God is omnipotent. Where is His Omnipotence if He cannot become a small child, a tiny insect or an atom? At our sweet will we can do practically nothing. But just because God is omnipotent, He can do anything He wants to do at His sweet Will: He can be vast, He can be infinitesimal.

God is everything, but each person has to feel for himself what God is for him. He can be infinite Light, infinite Consciousness, infinite Power, infinite Joy, infinite Bliss, infinite Compassion, infinite Energy. He can be personal, with form; again, he can be impersonal, without form, just as water has form when it is ice but no form when it is in the liquid state. At times we get joy when we see God with form; at times we get joy when we see God without form. We can see Him in His impersonal aspect as a vast expanse of Light. In his personal aspect He can appear as a luminous human being with two hands, two eyes and everything else that we have. He will be the most illumined Being here on earth and there in Heaven. When he appears as a personal Being, we can have all kinds of intimate talks with Him face to face.

Question: Some people claim not to believe in God, but they are still good people and they seem happy. How can you explain this?

Sri Chinmoy: No matter which way we appreciate the reality or want to identify ourselves with the reality, we have to feel that we are appreciating and identifying ourselves with Divinity; and this Divinity we call either God or Spirit or Being. If you do not want to call it God, you are at perfect liberty not to do so. But you have to call it happiness. Happiness itself is God. You can appreciate the beauty of nature and if you are happy, then the happiness that you are experiencing is God.

In one word, if God has to be defined, then I wish to say God is happiness.

Question: There are many people who claim that with the use of certain drugs they are able to get closer to God. How do you feel about using stimulants, drugs, etc., to stimulate the mind in order to get closer to God?

Sri Chinmoy: Let me start out by saying that there are two ways of approaching the Truth. One way is that by meditation and prayer, we know the real Truth, we feel the real ecstasy, we see the real Light, we experience Existence, Consciousness, Bliss. These last three go together and we can come into that state only through meditation and oneness with God. But those who are taking drugs are putting the cart before the horse. They are deceiving themselves into thinking that they already know the Truth. At the same time, they are not aware of the fact that by taking drugs, they are damaging their inner, spiritual faculties which are of paramount importance in order to enter into God's kingdom. Let me make it clear to you.

One can come closer to God only by loving God and meditating on God.

If you throw me into a sea and plunge me, immerse me forcibly in the water, not allowing me to come to the surface, then what shall I see? All blank, all white. And that is what actually happens to those who have taken to drugs. Through the effect of chemicals, a violent change of consciousness is effected. They get an experience... all white! Even if it is a higher experience, they cannot sustain it unless they take another dose of chemicals. But when I pray, when I concentrate, when I meditate, I enter into the Living Consciousness of God and I can learn to remain there. This is the positive and natural way of entering into God. God is natural and I am His son, you are His son; we have to follow the natural process. But by taking to drugs and using these artificial means, people are unconsciously, if not deliberately, negating the real Truth.

I have two or three students who used to take drugs. They have had first-hand 'experiences'. They tell me now that when they were taking drugs, it was nothing but self-delusion and self-annihilation. Now what they

43

experience is self-acceptance and self-fulfilment. So this is the difference that they have now discovered. Needless to say that I am proud of their present spiritual achievements.

To come back to your question, no man can come closer to God by taking drugs or stimulants. He can come closer to God only by loving God and meditating on God.

Question: Do drug experiences have any validity at all?

Sri Chinmoy: Drug experiences are like a false coin. It is as though you are a little child who has no money. Then you see a wonderful coin. You know it is a coin because you see the shape, and you are delighted that you have got some money so easily. But it is a false coin. If you bring it to a shopkeeper he will beat you or throw you out of the store. He will not accept it. You will find that your coin is worthless and you cannot buy anything with it.

Question: In terms of teaching, I have often faced problems explaining the Hindu doctrine of *maya*, especially in its understanding of life as 'illusory'. I have similar problems when I speak of the world as *lila* (God's Play) and try to emphasise the 'purposelessness' of God's created world as a consequence of its being God's Divine Play. How can I best teach these concepts to our students in the United States?

Sri Chinmoy: The Hindu doctrine uses the term *'maya'*, which means 'illusion'. It has been the Hindu belief, right from the very birth of the Hindu philosophy, that the world is an illusion. The Hindu spiritual figures, the Hindu philosophers and some of the Hindu thinkers get tremendous pleasure in telling the world that it is nothing but an illusion. Their philosophy is: why pay so much attention, or even any attention, to something that is unreal?

I wish to say that it is the height of our stupidity to say or feel that we have more wisdom or understanding than the Transcendental and Universal God. We are ready to pray to God. We are ready to devote ourselves to our idea of

Him, but we are not ready to accept God's creation as something real. If we believe that we are praying to a God who is real, then how can we separate God's reality from God?

Maya has another meaning. It means 'fleeting, impermanent, temporary'. The things that we see or we do or we are in the physical world do not last permanently. Therefore, some people describe the physical world as unreal. But the outer reality does not require immortality. Although the highest reality is infinite, eternal and immortal, reality can also be short-lived, just as infinity can be infinitely tiny as well as infinitely vast. Reality can be short-lived and reality can be long-term. Again, reality can be immortal. A flower that lasts only for a day is not unreal. A human being who lives for 80 years is not unreal. They are temporary; therefore, you might describe them as illusory. They are real, but limited, impermanent.

> No matter how hard we try to define God, we cannot. To define is to limit, and God is without limits. God is Eternity's Child playing in His own Infinity's Heart-Garden.

Some philosophers are of the opinion that only that which lasts forever is real. But if God's Will is to create something permanent or to create something that will last only for a short time, that is His choice. Both things are still His creations. He is at once the Creator and the creation, the Player and the play, the impersonal and the personal, the invisible and the visible, the known and the unknown, the real and the unreal.

No matter how hard we try to define God, we cannot. To define is to limit, and God is without limits. God is Eternity's Child playing in His own Infinity's Heart-Garden.

As a little child gets satisfaction, abundant satisfaction, when he plays with his friends, even so, God the Child-Player likes to play with His child-friend-creations. God is one, but He wants to enjoy Himself in countless ways and in countless forms. And He does this through His Cosmic Play, through His *lila*. You and I and all of your students are God's creation-friends, although we may not understand the purpose of God's creation or our role in it.

Question: What should one's attitude be towards things that one did before, when one's higher mind, knowing it was wrong, was not in control? What should be one's attitude towards guilt resulting from these former actions?

Sri Chinmoy: One's attitude at that time should be that the past is buried in oblivion. You have done something wrong. If you cherish the idea of guilt, "I have done something wrong," you are being sincere, but thinking of your mistake, having this sincerity, does not help. Yes, you have done something wrong. But by having a guilty consciousness, you do not get light or wisdom. You have done something that is not right. Then, try to do the right thing, the divine thing. This second, this minute you have used. You could have used it either for a right purpose or a wrong purpose. All right, you have used it for a wrong purpose. Then use the following minute for a divine purpose, and if you use it for a divine purpose without thinking of the previous minute when you did something wrong, then what happens? Your positive strength, this will-power you have used to do the right thing will then have the power in entirety, in fullness. But, if you think of the past minute with a sense of guilt, that you have done something wrong, and then you think that the following minute you are determined to do the right thing, half of your power is again lost in darkness and only half can be utilised for the following minute of right action. So, I tell my disciples to try to bring to the fore their full power in the following minute and nullify the previous mistake.

If one cherishes or broods over misdeeds, then one is again strengthening one's own guilt unconsciously. I may think, "I am repenting." But why should I repent? I have done something wrong. I am a hero; I am ready to face the consequences. If I have done something wrong, then I have the capacity to do the thing right. Again, by focusing all the attention on the right thing, we are adding to our positive strength.

The sense of guilt, the constant feeling of self-reproach is, unfortunately, all-pervading in the Western world. If my Source is God, the Absolute Infinite Light, if I know that it is from there that I came, then some day I must go back to my Source. During my stay on earth I got, unfortunately, some unhealthy, unaspiring and destructive experiences. Now, I have to get rid of these unfortunate experiences. I have to get fulfilling experiences in my life. So for that I have to concentrate only on the right thing, the divine thing which will fulfil me, and not on the things that have stood in my way.

Delight and divine consciousness

There is a great difference between pleasure and joy. What is actually happening is that the human world, the outer consciousness, is crying for pleasure; and each time pleasure is fulfilled, we see that frustration looms large in our pleasure. But, if we feel that joy is coming into our lives, then joy grows from joy into more joy, abundant joy, boundless joy. So, when there is real joy within us — when we meditate for five minutes or ten minutes — we get inner joy that fulfils us. But, when we think of pleasure, of buying something unnecessary like a Cadillac or something of that sort, we are fulfilling our pleasure there. Soon after, we are frustrated because the one we have got is not big enough; we want something more comfortable. We are running after comfort here. If we run after comfort with the help of our desire, then naturally we will not be satisfied. But, if we cry for joy, inner joy, then each time we run towards fulfilment because inner joy wants us only to fulfil God; and only by fulfilling God can we be really fulfilled.

There is a general notion that if we go through suffering, tribulations and physical pain then our system will be purified. This idea is not founded upon reality. There are many people who are suffering because of their past karma or because undivine forces are attacking them, but we cannot say that they are nearing their destination No! They have to aspire more sincerely in order to reach their destination. We shall not welcome pain; we shall try to conquer pain if it appears. If we can take pain as an experience, then we can try to transform it into joy by our own identification with joy, which we then try to bring into the pain itself.

Physical pain, vital pain and mental pain have to be transformed into joy through our constant inner cry for something that will give us real and permanent satisfaction. In the spiritual life the best thing is to take pain as an experience which has to be transformed into an experience of joy. Joy is the only eternal reality, the only permanent and everlasting reality. But it is absolutely wrong to say that each time we suffer we go one step ahead toward our goal.

There are some people who feel that pain is indispensable, but it is not necessary to go through suffering before we can enter into the kingdom of Delight. Many people have realised God through love. The Father has love for the child and the child has love for the Father. This love takes us to our goal. Our philosophy emphasises the positive way of approaching Truth. We have limited light; now let us increase it. Let us progress from more light to abundant light to infinite Light.

> The highest discovery is this: we came from Delight, we are in Delight, we grow in Delight and at the end of our journey's close we retire into Delight.

Delight is now in the inner world. The outer world is all suffering. We see people quarrelling and fighting. We have many undivine elements in us: fear, doubt, anxiety, worry and so forth. But when we go deep within, on the strength of our highest meditation, we discover that Delight was our origin, our Source. In Delight we play the cosmic Game and at the end of the cosmic Game we again retire into Delight.

Lower and higher worlds

Deep inside us there are seven lower worlds and seven higher worlds. We are trying to transform the lower worlds into luminous worlds, worlds of perfection; and, at the same time, we are trying to bring the higher worlds into outer manifestation. Some of the higher worlds we already see operating in our physical world, on earth. First comes the physical, then the vital, then the mind, then the plane of intuition or the intuitive mind, then the overmind and the supermind. After the supermind comes Existence-Consciousness-Bliss — *Sat-Chit-Ananda*.

If you know how to observe them, you can see that some of these worlds are already functioning in you. During meditation, you can clearly see that it is not the physical world that you are entering into. It is something else: the higher mind or the overmind, or intuition or some other subtle world. But only spiritual Masters and great aspirants are conscious of the fact that these worlds are manifesting in their day-to-day activities, in the outer world itself. The ordinary person, even when flashes of intuition enter into his mind, will not be able to know that they are coming from the world of intuition. But each person, either today or tomorrow, has to become conscious of these worlds. Not only that, but also he has to manifest the truth, the light, the beauty, the wealth of all the higher worlds in this world.

Great spiritual Masters from time immemorial have brought down the *Sat* and *Chit* aspects. But *Ananda* is much more difficult to bring down. Some could not bring it at all. Some brought it, but it lasted for only a few seconds or a few minutes and then went back up again.

> *Peace is accessible; we can bring down Peace. Light and Power can easily be brought down. But the Delight which immortalises our inner and outer consciousness has not yet been established on earth.*

Peace is accessible; we can bring down Peace. Light and Power can easily be brought down. But the Delight which immortalises our inner and outer consciousness has not yet been established on earth. It comes and then goes away because it sees so much imperfection in the earth-atmosphere that it cannot remain.

Even spiritually advanced people are often confused. They feel an inner ecstasy which comes from the vital world, and they think this is the real Delight. But it is not so. Real Delight comes from the highest world to the soul, and from the soul it saturates the whole being.

This *Ananda* is absorbed differently from physical delight, or what we call pleasure or enjoyment. The supramental Delight is totally different from the world of pleasure and enjoyment. Once you get even an iota of it, you feel your entire inner being dancing for joy like a child with utmost purity, and your outer being feels true Immortality in its outer existence. If you get this Delight even for a second, you will remember it all your life.

All around us is the cosmic Game, the cosmic Play. The universe is full of joy, inner joy and outer joy. When realisation takes place, we have to feel the necessity of manifesting this constant Delight in our heart. This Delight glows, but does not actually burn. It has tremendous intensity, but it is all softness and absolutely sweet-flowing Nectar. One day I brought it down into my gross physical, so that when I was smiling, at that time I was scattering the highest Delight to each of you. But I must say that it has all disappeared. There is nobody among the disciples who has kept any of it.

GOD AND THE HIGHER WORLDS

Question: If any human being can so transform his consciousness as to identify with the Universal Consciousness, certainly this human being deserves to be revered. At the same time, you have madmen who go around posing as elevated beings. What then are the distinguishing marks between a saint and a madman?

Sri Chinmoy: Saints are intoxicated with the divine ecstasy. Great spiritual saints, when they attain their spiritual perfection are drinking ambrosial nectar. They are living in that delightful consciousness in which they feel that the world itself is holding the spiritual ocean of bliss. Some of them try to bring down that highest Delight, *Ananda*, from a very high plane where they have received it, and sometimes they find it difficult. When they find it difficult to touch the material plane carrying this Bliss, they may lose their inner balance and for a short time become forgetful of the physical consciousness. At that time they may not be able to function normally on the physical plane. A seeker may forget his name, for example, and others may say he is acting like a madman.

But an ordinary madman is mentally, vitally or physically dislocated. He never knows what he should do or what he should say or how he should act. He has permanently lost the connection between the physical world and his own existence on earth. So whenever he says or does something, there is no harmony with the Universal Consciousness. That is to say, he cannot project himself into the Universal Consciousness in which we are all abiding. All of us are living in the Universal Consciousness, although we may not be conscious of it. At the same time, we are not violating the rules of the Universal Consciousness. A madman is also unaware of the Universal Consciousness, but at the same time, he is violating the laws of the universe, the Universal Consciousness, owing to his ignorance.

As we have preconceived ideas, the madman too has preconceived ideas, but he cannot formulate his ideas as we formulate ours. We have got a brain; we know our mind. We know how one thought can follow another thought. In a madman's case, it is not like that. All the thoughts and ideas of the higher and lower worlds come into him in a flash, and he loses all his inner and outer balance. The forces and the pressures of the other worlds enter into him and get a free channel in him to express themselves.

An ordinary madman will never open to the Light or the Truth or that which can save him, his life, his very existence on earth; whereas the God-intoxicated madman, who is the true saint, is mad with the divine Beauty, the divine Light, the divine Purity and all that is divine. He wants to possess and to be possessed by Divinity itself. This is the difference between an ordinary madman and a God-intoxicated saint.

The God-intoxicated madman, who is the true saint, is mad with the divine Beauty, the divine Light, the divine Purity and all that is divine.

God is man's eternal Friend. When man approaches God, not as a beggar, but as a friend, he gets God sooner. He gets God in His sweetest Form. We are not God's slaves. We are His children, His chosen children.

CHAPTER SEVEN

Kundalini Yoga, the chakras and occult power

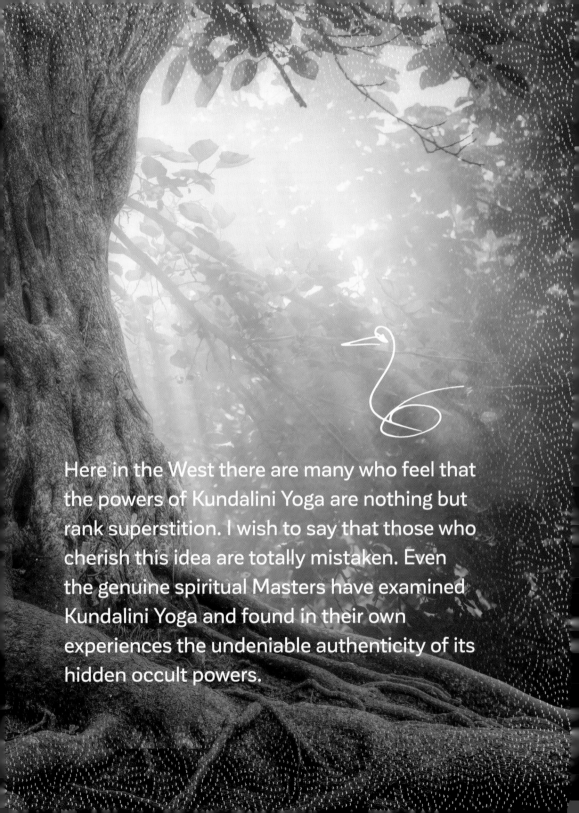

Here in the West there are many who feel that the powers of Kundalini Yoga are nothing but rank superstition. I wish to say that those who cherish this idea are totally mistaken. Even the genuine spiritual Masters have examined Kundalini Yoga and found in their own experiences the undeniable authenticity of its hidden occult powers.

Kundalini, the Yoga of purity

Kundalini is a process of Yoga. Yoga means conscious union with God. Inside our subtle body there are six major psychic centres (*chakras*). When we open these centres, we get occult powers. The process that we follow in order to open them is called kundalini, or Kundalini Yoga.

There are various paths that lead to the Goal. Kundalini is one path that offers special power, but there are other paths which also offer similar powers. Let us say there are three roads leading towards the same destination. One road has quite a few trees and flowers, the second has a few trees and flowers and the third one does not have any at all. While walking the kundalini path, you see some power, but this power is definitely not the ultimate power. For those who have no spiritual or occult power, kundalini power seems very vast. But in comparison to the power of the Goal, kundalini power is nothing.

On some paths, this kind of occult power is not there. The road is clear and you just go forward and reach the Goal. Then, once you reach the Goal, you get the omnipotent power, spiritual power. But the follower of kundalini often just stays with his limited power. On very rare occasions seekers have fallen from the spiritual path because they have achieved spiritual power. Kundalini power, occult power, has taken many, many sincere seekers away from the Truth.

Most of the time, kundalini power is a curse and not a blessing. If you misuse kundalini power, then you are ruined. You destroy all your possibilities to realise the Highest and God knows how many incarnations it will take you to come back to the right path again. Ninety-nine percent of the time the kundalini power is misused. But if you properly use it, then you get inspiration to do something good for the world.

Some people very often make a mistake. They try to raise their kundalini in the traditional way, starting from the base of their spine; but their vital remains impure. Then they get into a lot of vital trouble. They say, "Oh, before Yoga I was far better off. I was very pure, but now my purity has all gone."

If one opens up the chakras without purification of the vital, especially the lower vital, then one can become unbalanced, mad, insane. Many people go crazy when they open up the chakras before purification takes place. Awakening the kundalini power without first being purified is like giving a child a knife. There is every possibility of his misusing it. He may cut his finger or do something most harmful and damaging. But if one is grown up and mature, then he will use the knife to cut fruit and offer it to his friends.

If one really wants to learn occultism, two things have to be totally shunned. I am talking of strict occultism, not black magic and all that, which anyone can practise. The two things to be shunned are fear and sex. If there is any fear, either in the physical or in the mental or in the psychic, then the great dynamic occult powers can never be developed. And if there are lower vital movements, sex indulgence and impure thoughts in the being, then no occult power can enter.

If you wish to follow the path of kundalini, my humble advice to you is to first try to awaken the heart centre. The heart centre is considerably pure. The vital or disturbing emotions will be purified by the opening of this centre. If you can first open up the heart centre and from there take the purity and enter into the lower centres, then there is no danger.

If you wish to follow the path of kundalini, my humble advice to you is to first try to awaken the heart centre.

Kundalini Yoga is the Yoga of absolute purity. It is one of the most sacred Yogas and physical, vital, mental and psychic purity is of paramount importance. The three major nerves — *ida*, *pingala* and *sushumna* — will suffer immensely and immediately if there is any sexual indulgence. And it is not only physical relations that are bad. If somebody enjoys lower vital thoughts, impure thoughts, in the mind, that is also harmful.

So we have to know when it is advisable for us to awaken the kundalini power.

In all Yogas you need a spiritual teacher. In Kundalini Yoga, the need for a spiritual teacher is paramount. If you follow other Yogas, you undoubtedly need a Master; but if you do not care for a Master, if you want to go slowly, steadily, like an Indian bullock cart, there is no harm. There is no danger involved in other paths. You will reach your destination only after thousands of years, in another life, but there is no particular danger in your travelling without a guide. But in Kundalini Yoga, if you do not have a real Master to teach you, then you are playing with fire. If the spiritual centres, especially the lower centres — *muladhara, svadhisthana* and *manipura* — are opened untimely, without full preparation, they can create untold misery for the seeker. The teacher uses his vast wisdom to shorten the long road for the student. The teacher uses his deep compassion to transform the arduous road into an easy and smooth road for the student. The teacher uses his illumining light to remove uncertainty from the mind of the student and replace it with absolute certainty. The teacher uses his indomitable power to cast aside all danger to the student from the journey's start to the journey's close. He also makes the path a sunlit path, so that the student can run the fastest without danger or obstruction on the way.

Occult power is quite often
Drastic and volcanic.
Spiritual power is always pure
And absolutely sure.

Question: Which of the seven chakras is most important for the beginner to open first?

Sri Chinmoy: One should try to open the heart chakra, or spiritual centre, first. This is not only for the beginner but for everyone who practises the spiritual life and who wants to open the chakras. The Sanskrit term for this chakra is Anahata, the Soundless Sound. Its seed sound is Yam; this is its secret name. But you need not use the word yam; you can chant 'Supreme' or 'God'. Some people get more joy when they utter the name of God, the Supreme. In your case, 'Supreme' would be the best to use if you want to open this chakra. When this chakra opens, it gives you a sense of Joy, Peace and Bliss. The outer emotions, vital emotions or disturbing emotions, will be purified by the opening of this centre. For beginner or for anyone who wants to open the chakras, it is best to open the heart chakra first.

CHAPTER EIGHT

True and false Masters

Following a spiritual Master is like walking with someone who is infinitely stronger than you and is always ready to help you and make you happy in a divine way.

The role of a spiritual teacher

Everyone has a Guru, the real Guru, and that is the Inner Pilot, the Pilot Supreme. There is only one Guru and that Guru is God. A spiritual Master is only a representative of God. When one is a beginner, one cannot or may not know where the real Guru, the eternal Guru, is, just because he does not have a conscious and free access to Him. At this point, if somebody helps the seeker enter into his own world of Divinity and Reality, then the seeker learns or discovers his own Divinity. This is the role of the spiritual Master, the human Guru. But the real Guru is inside the inmost recesses of each aspiring heart.

A spiritual teacher is the eldest member in the family. Just because he has a little more Peace, Light and Bliss than others, God has chosen him to give his little Peace, Light and Bliss to his younger brothers and sisters. He knows that he is not the father. And, also, his younger brothers and sisters know that he is not the father. The father is somebody else. But because he is the elder brother, he is supposed to know where the father is. The elder brother of the family tells the younger ones, "Come, I will show you where our Father is." And once he can bring the younger ones to their common Father, his role is over. They will be on their own as soon as he shows them where the Father is.

Spirituality is not an easy thing. If one wants to learn it well, one should take help. You went to college and university to get your highest diploma; then you gave up your studies and started your own life.

If the seeker does not take help, then he may have some difficulties, some serious doubts about his own spiritual life, and then he will give up. He will think that it is impossible for him to practise spirituality, since there are so many doubts and so many wrong things in his life. But if there is a spiritual Master, the Master will always encourage him and help him.

So it is good to have a spiritual Master, but it is not obligatory. There are many who have realised God without having spiritual Masters. But if you get a good one, it is very good; you are lucky.

There are quite a few ways to know whether a Master is genuine or not. If the Master says that he will be able to grant you realisation overnight, then he is a false Master. If he says that if you give him a fee of a few hundred or a few thousand dollars, then he will be able to help you enter into a higher realm of consciousness and attain Peace, Light and Bliss, then he is a false Master. A true Master will tell the seeker all the time that he is not God; he is not even the Guru. God Himself is the real Master. The human Master is only serving God in the seekers; he is not the Guru. The real Guru is God Himself. So if a seeker wants to know who a true Master is, from these guidelines he can usually know the real from the false.

The genuine Master, the genuine seeker

Very often people come and try to judge whether the Master is perfect or not. Here they can easily make a mistake. If the Master is genuine — that is to say, if the Master has realised God — then what may appear to them to be weaknesses in the Master will not hinder them in their self-realisation.

Again, so-called human weaknesses are one thing; but if the Master indulges in lower vital life, sex life, then that Master is very bad and you have to leave him. If you don't feel purity in the Master, if you don't see in him the perfection of the lower vital life, the emotional life, then you must give a wide berth to him. Otherwise, how will you ever get from him the perfection of your own vital life?

Question: How can a person recognise a genuine spiritual Master?

Sri Chinmoy: When you meditate with a spiritual Master, if out of his infinite kindness he wants to show you Light and Peace through his eyes or through his spiritual presence, he can do so. When a real spiritual Master looks at a genuine aspirant, the aspirant is bound to feel something in him. A God-realised man or spiritual Master is not someone with wings and a halo to identify him. He is normal, except that in his inner life he has abundant Peace,

Light and Bliss. So if you come to a spiritual man expecting something other than boundless Peace, Light, Bliss and Power, then you will be disappointed.

But again, you must know if you are fit to judge. If I know nothing about medical science, how am I going to judge a great doctor? Only another doctor will know how to judge him properly. But a nurse, who knows a little about medical science, can appreciate a great doctor far better than I. In the spiritual life, a real seeker who has sincere aspiration and dedication has already achieved a little bit of inner Light. Because of his aspiration, God has endowed him with an iota of Light, and with that Light, he is bound to see and feel something in a true spiritual Master. If one is really advanced in the spiritual life and is making fast progress in his inner journey, then his aspiration will be the best judge as to whether the other person, the so-called spiritual Master, is genuine or not. So the best judge is one's sincere aspiration.

A spiritual Master is he Who is a tireless guide To God-searching Human beings.

An unrealised Master can fool you for a day or for a month or for a few years, but he cannot fool you forever. If your own sincere aspiration is one hundred percent pure and you want nothing but God, then God will not keep you with an insincere, unrealised Master indefinitely. It is impossible!

There is a great difference between an occultist and a real spiritual Master, who follows the path of surrender to God's Will. "Let Thy Will be done" is not only the Christ's message; it is the message of all spiritual Masters. "Let Thy Will be done" is the essence of the yoga of surrender. There is no spiritual Master who will not come to this realisation. But the occultist, if he is not of the highest order, will feel that his own will should be done first. This is the difference between an occultist and a real spiritual Master.

The Son of God, Jesus Christ, was on earth for thirty-three years. Only during the last three years of his life did he perform miracles. But do you think the world still adores and worships him just because he could walk on water or resurrect a dead man? No, it is not because of his miracles that he is still worshipped, but because he brought down the eternal Consciousness, the infinite Consciousness. Sri Ramakrishna performed practically no miracles and there were many, many other spiritual Masters who did not do miracles. They felt that performing miracles on the physical plane would be childlike in comparison to what they were capable of doing on the spiritual plane, in the heart's region, where infinite Peace, Light and Bliss abide.

Kundalini power and all the miraculous powers on earth are fleeting, for they are earth-bound powers. But the Power of the Self is infinite; the Power of the transcendental Self is infinite and immortal. The most important thing on earth for a spiritual seeker is the awakening of the consciousness and the realisation of the Self, for this is eternal. If somebody comes here and performs some miracles, we will be fascinated. But the moment we go home there will be nothing to sustain our faith in what he has done. It seems to be all magic and trickery. And how long can we cherish the magician inside us or before us? But when somebody lifts up our consciousness even for a second, or if we ourselves do it on the strength of our intense aspiration, then our faith in that experience lasts, because it is our own inner experience.

> *Anything that lasts forever we need. It is Immortality, inner Immortality that we need; and this comes through the awakening and elevation of our consciousness.*

CHAPTER NINE

Spirituality and society

When the power of love
Replaces the love of power,
Man will have a new name:
God.

The world situation

It is my inner feeling that the world is progressing. I do not encourage pessimistic ideas, thoughts and so forth. God Himself is inspiring the world, it is His Creation. He is not doomed to disappointment, far from it. He looks at His Creation and He sees that it needs encouragement, inspiration and guidance. When we create something, we try to make it better and more illumining and fulfilling. Even so, God has created His Creation and now He is trying to make it more beautiful, more fruitful. So the world is progressing. We are all trying to become better instruments of God.

Question: There are a lot of people who would suggest that the world situation is fairly tense right now.

Sri Chinmoy: That story we have heard right from the beginningless past! Four hundred years ago, if you read any history book, you will see that they said the world was going to end and people were not nice. You can start even from the Vedic era. Everybody, from the beginning of Creation, will say this world is not divine. All right, it is not divine. Now also it is not divine, but the fact is that we are using the terms 'divine' and 'perfect'. That means we have an inner urge to become perfect.

Our philosophy is to move forward. Once a sprinter leaves the starting blocks, he does not come back. He has to go forward until he reaches the goal.

When the very idea of goodness enters into our mind, that means we want to become good.

Our philosophy is to move forward. Once a sprinter leaves the starting blocks, he does not come back. He has to go forward until he reaches the goal.

Individual perfection is of paramount importance. The world will never be perfect unless and until each individual in the world has become perfect. We cannot expect the whole world to be perfect overnight. But if we can achieve inner perfection individually, then the world's outer perfection will gradually grow. First we have to solve our own problems — that is to say, we have to achieve our own illumination. If we have inner illumination ourselves, then only we can spread it. But if we say, "Oh, the world is so vast, what difference will one individual's illumination make?" then we are making a mistake. One will be illumined today, two tomorrow and so on. Slowly, steadily and unerringly we are trying to manifest the divinity within us. What we need is infinite patience. Let us have that patience, which is the light of our ever-expanding consciousness.

Question: Should we concern ourselves with the world if the world is going downhill and we are trying to climb uphill?

Sri Chinmoy: In order to lift somebody, you have to be one inch higher than he is. If you feel that you are secure, then lift up the world. If you are not secure and you try to lift up someone else, then he will pull you down.

Question: How is it that the spiritual force is so strong, yet the world seems to be such a disastrous place?

Sri Chinmoy: The spiritual force is strong, but how many people are accepting it? How many people want it? Out of all the millions of people in New York how many are aspiring? Unaspiring people are infinitely more in number than those who are aspiring. Only when the divine force is accepted and embraced by the majority will the undivine forces in the world begin to diminish. Most of us have accepted darkness as natural and normal, which is absolutely wrong. We should try to feel that light is normal and natural, and that the unlit forces, the physical forces and the vital forces that we employ, are the abnormal and unnatural ones.

I have not come here to bring about any social change. I have come to the West only to bring light, to be of service to people, only to bring to the fore what is real in you.

If the real comes to the fore in you, in him, in her, in everybody, then you will see some significant changes in society.

Society is like a house. If all the members of the house become perfect, then the house will flow with peace, light and harmony. It is from individual progress that the collective progress comes. If I become perfect, if you become perfect, if everybody becomes perfect, then you will see that the social changes will be unnecessary. But if we try to make society perfect when it is still full of imperfect human beings, we will sadly fail.

War and peace

There are two wars, the inner and the outer. The inner war is the war that our inner being or the soul fights against limitations, ignorance, doubt and death. The outer war is the war that man fights with man, nation fights with nation, country fights with country. Now the question is: when and how can these wars come to an end? These wars can come to an end only when the inner war first stops. That is to say, when in the inner world, the inner being or the soul conquers ignorance, fear, doubt and death. Then in the outer world there

The outer war will come to an end when the inner war is resolved, when the inner war stops. Both wars will come to an end and are bound to end in the process of human evolution.

will be no necessity to wage war. We fight because deep inside us there is disharmony, there is fear, there is anxiety and there is aggression. When deep within us there is peace, joy, plenitude and fulfilment, we shall not invite war.

The outer world needs peace. Now, how can we have outer peace? Can we have that peace by making friends with the whole world? No. We may have many friends, even true friends, bosom friends, but that does not mean that we will have peace in the outer world. I assure you that even if the whole outer world becomes friendship itself and everyone is ready to offer help, there will be no peace in the outer world. Outer peace will come into existence only when we discover inner peace. This inner peace is something which we already have. It is not something that we have to invent; it is something we have to discover.

If this inner peace is not brought to the fore, then man can never have peace in the outer life. If the inner peace does not come to the fore and make the outer circumstances peaceful, the peace that we may see in the outer life will be like a counterfeit coin. Friendship, amity and harmony in society will not have an abiding substance if the inner peace is wanting.

Peace itself is strength. When you have inner peace, you can have joy and delight when you enter into the outer world. The outer world can be under your control when you have peace of mind, even if you have only a little peace of mind. Wherever you go, you will make your own peace. If you do not have any inner peace to offer, the only qualities you will express are restlessness, aggression and other undivine things.

Peace itself is strength. The outer world can be under your control when you have peace of mind.

The world is something very huge, but each person represents the world. You and I create the world by the vibrations that we offer to the world. Any little room, let us say, is a miniature world. If we can invoke peace and then offer it to somebody else, we will see how peace expands from one to two persons, and gradually to the world at large.

Theory and practice must go together. When we pray and meditate, we develop or acquire peace of mind, let us say. When we have peace of mind, then we can come into the outer world to solve our problems. The outer world is full of problems, but our inner world is inundated with peace. How can we get in touch with this inner peace? That we do on the strength of our prayer and meditation.

Early in the morning we pray and meditate to acquire some inner wealth: peace, joy and bliss. Then, we go out to our respective offices and mix with our friends or colleagues. Because we pray and meditate, no matter what happens or what we do, we remain unperturbed; we remain calm and quiet. The inner life we practice through our prayer and meditation, and the outer life we practice through our dedication to the cause of humanity.

Question: **You have offered meditations at the United Nations, and you have a fine reputation for that. So let me ask you some questions about problems of world conflict. Why do we see so much strife around us in the world? Why are many nations in conflict with each other, and why do people not get along because of different religions or races or economic points of view?**

Sri Chinmoy: It is because we are swimming in the sea of ignorance. Each individual has limitations, each individual has darkness, each individual has obscurity and impurity. Each individual feels that by becoming superior to others he will derive happiness. Each individual feels a sense of separation. Each individual feels that so long as he can maintain his individuality, he will remain happy. But this is absurd. Happiness comes from oneness. You and I must become inseparably one in order to become happy. But the world does not believe in that kind of happiness. The world wants separation, although separation ends in frustration, and frustration ends in destruction.

It is very difficult to achieve oneness. Even in our own being there is often conflict. Sometimes the mind wants to do something and the physical revolts or the vital revolts. The heart wants to do something and the other parts of our being revolt. In our own personal existence we have no harmony, so how can we expect to have peace on earth?

Again, if we pray and meditate, God is bound to listen to our prayer. He is omniscient, omnipotent and omnipresent, and He is all Love. He will grant us His boundless Love and, on the strength of His boundless Love, we will be able to see the whole world and each individual in the world as our own, very own.

It is lack of prayer and meditation that causes this problem of separativity. If we pray soulfully and meditate soulfully, then this problem can easily be solved. At that time there will be a world without conflict, without war, without misunderstanding. There will be a world of oneness, satisfaction and perfection. This world of oneness, satisfaction and perfection can dawn only when we want to go to the Source and become part and parcel of the Source.

Peace does not mean the absence of war. Peace means the presence of harmony, love, satisfaction and oneness. Peace means a flood of love in the world-family.

Patriotism

From the spiritual point of view, patriotism is love of one's own country, love of one's source. Your parents are your source; in the same way, your country is also your source. As a soul, you were staying in the soul's region. Then you wanted to take human incarnation and you needed a country.

> Patriotism is a golden opportunity for an individual to work together with his dearest motherland.

The place that invoked your soul, the place that out of love, out of joy, out of kindness and concern agreed to accept you as its very own, that place deserves your heart's and soul's adoration while you are in the body. Patriotism is self-enlargement, self-expansion and, at the same time, self-giving to the source. This self-enlargement takes place in the divine way; it is not enlargement of ego. The self-giving and self-offering of patriotism come from the feeling that other countries can derive some light from your own country's awakening.

Patriotism is self-giving and self-expansion based on your conscious oneness with all consciousness, your inseparable oneness with all. That is the meaning of patriotism in the spiritual sense.

Patriotism is undivine only if there is no real sincere feeling behind patriotism, if in the name of patriotism you just go and condemn or strike other nations and try to lord it over them. It is fanatic patriotism if you say that you and your country are by far the best, that there is no nation which is pure, divine and spiritual except yours. If you feel that only you and your nation exist, that others are all bad, undivine and impure, that only your country represents truth and God and that the rest of the countries are all bad — if you have that kind of patriotic feeling, then it is really undivine.

From patriotism, from the feeling of nationalism, we go to internationalism. To a child, his mother is his whole world. He discovers his whole world in his mother and father. For a few years his parents are his main concern and then his high school, his college and the town or city where he lives. Then he feels that the nation is his whole world. All the time his vision is increasing. When he widens his vision, he sees that the whole world belongs to him. Then he hears the word 'spiritual', and he feels not only the necessity of progress inside his own house but also the necessity of world progress.

In this way, starting with nationalism, one eventually progresses to an international feeling. But if I do not love my nation, I am not going to love other nations. One can and must go from the one to the many.

Question: I read that the soul has no nationality. What do you mean when you say a soul is Indian or British or Russian or some other nationality?

Sri Chinmoy: I was born into a Hindu family, so you can call me a Hindu. Another person is Muslim and a third person is Christian. But when we pray and meditate, we enter into the Universal Consciousness, and this Universal Consciousness becomes part and parcel of our life. At that time, there is no Hinduism or Islam or Christianity; there is only oneness.

You can say you were born in Russia; so you are a Russian soul. But as you gain inner experience and become more spiritually developed, you will say that you belong not only to Russia but to the Soviet Union. Then gradually you will say that you belong to the whole world. I was born in Bengal; so I am Bengali. Bengal is in India; so I am an Indian. India is in Asia; so I am an Asian. Asia is a continent in the world; so I belong to the whole world. I am a citizen of the whole world.

Each individual is consciously or unconsciously making progress. On the strength of that progress, the individual soul sees and feels its oneness with others. You can call me a Bengali. But because of my inner realisation, I can say that I am cosmopolitan the same way Socrates said he belonged to the entire world.

Science and technology

Question: Is technology acting as a hindrance to God-realisation?

Sri Chinmoy: The answer is in the affirmative as well as in the negative. When modern technology is serving as an expression of the inner soul, when it feels that it has a connecting link with the inner life, the inner existence, at that time technology is a help to God-realisation. But very often we see that technology and the inner life do not go together. The outer world with its success is running towards a different goal. We have to be very careful about this, for no matter how much success we derive from technology, the infinite fulfilment cannot take place if the soul is not there. Again, the soul is lame if the outer life does not keep pace with it through technological and scientific progress.

For the absolute fulfilment of God's Vision and Reality here on earth, science and spirituality must go together.

Science and spirituality have to go together, either today or in the distant future. Now they are at daggers drawn. But for the absolute fulfilment of God's Vision and Reality here on earth, science and spirituality must go together.

From spirituality we can expect liberation and realisation. From technology and science we can expect material perfection — the material embodiment of the highest Truth. When realisation is inside material success, only then will the material world achieve permanence in eternal values. Again, if perfection is lacking in the inner world, then the material success has to inspire the inner realisation to come and take the lead.

Question: What is your opinion about television?

Sri Chinmoy: Except for the news, if you ask me the percentage of television that is good, I will say only two percent is a blessing. Ninety-eight percent of television is a curse, a hostile force. And a day will come when people will agree with me about how far the computer and scientific research have also taken the heart from their life. In the world of the heart, they have become bankrupt.

The material world is good, to a certain extent. It expedites material prosperity. But no matter how rich we become in the material sense, God-realisation will never, never come from material success, material achievements. The two can go side by side, but God-realisation itself can only come from the inner life, the spiritual life.

If I want to know all about world history, then I have to study history. Geography will be of no avail. Similarly, those who want to study science will go in that direction. But I do not think that one day science or computer technology will come forward and say, "This is God. He is standing in front of you." If this were ever the case, then all the spiritual Masters would have to come back from Heaven and surrender to the computer.

The computer
Unimaginably shortens
My outer journey.

The computer
Unpardonably lengthens
My inner journey.

CHAPTER TEN

The end of the world, evil forces, and the origin of mankind

From the strict
spiritual point of view
there is no such thing
as evil.

The immortal consciousness

The world is full of imagination. God has been very kind to us; He has given us imagination in infinite measure. Neither California nor Puerto Rico nor any part of the world is going to be dissolved. It is simply absurd and impossible, even if the astrologers say so. But this rumour creates great sensation. As for parts of the land sinking into the sea, well, there is always the possibility of this kind of change in the earth's surface, but it cannot be predicted with any accuracy by astrologers, since there are always forces working which they cannot evaluate.

The world is very vast. The universe is very vast. Nothing can totally destroy it. Human consciousness cannot be destroyed, not even by the atom bomb.

But why do we have to think of whether a particular place will last or not? Let us think of our own realisation. God-realisation is our Goal. To wonder whether this or that place will continue to exist will not help us in reaching our Goal. If we can remain in God's Consciousness we are immortal, but if we remain in the earth-consciousness we will not be immortal. It is the divinized consciousness that makes us immortal, and not the place where we live.

Question: Does evil exist?

Sri Chinmoy: From the strict spiritual point of view there is no such thing as evil. Only when we remain in the world of relativity, in the ordinary human consciousness, do we say that this is evil and this is divine. If we go deep within, we see that there are a few things with less light and there are a few things with more light. Things that have little light or practically no light we call evil. And things that have considerable light we call divine.

Each individual has divinity within him. But his divinity has not come to the fore and fully manifested itself. Each individual also has undivine qualities to some extent. His undivine qualities can be transcended, illumined, perfected and transformed into the divine qualities that he already has.

When we use the term 'evil,' our mind immediately looks down upon the reality and has a superior feeling. But if we say something right now embodies light in infinitesimal measure, then we get the opportunity, the inspiration, the aspiration to transform it into something divine. So the best thing is to say a limited light is operating in the existence or the reality which we call evil. Then we will try to transform the limited light into abundant light.

Question: Are accidents caused by evil forces, or is there just something in the universe that causes things accidentally?

Sri Chinmoy: There are evil forces all around us. Sometimes these evil forces can cause accidents. Again, sometimes a lack of concentration, or the forces within us, can result in accidents.

Question: What can we do to protect ourselves against the evil forces?

Sri Chinmoy: Regular prayer and meditation is the only way. It is as if we know that we have an enemy. Let us say that we have to go out in the morning. We cannot stay inside our house all the time, it is impossible. But we have to feel that we are well protected the moment we leave the house. Sometimes if our prayer and meditation are not very solid or profound, the forces may attack and do a little harm. But if there is no prayer or meditation at all, then all protection is lost.

Again, gratitude is a form of prayer, a form of protection. If we offer gratitude to the Supreme early in the morning, then immediately gratitude itself will hold protection for us. We are not asking for protection. We are offering gratitude because God has done something for us. The moment we offer our gratitude, God expands our receptivity. When He expands our receptivity, immediately Light enters into us. The function of Light is to enter into us. Light waits at every second to enter into us. And the moment we are receptive, the moment we expand our power of receptivity, it enters. Our receptivity is like a vessel. The bigger we can make it, the more it can contain.

Question: Where did human beings come from? Did they come from Adam and Eve, or from the monkeys?

There is no shadow of doubt that Matter and Spirit are one. Spirit, when it is fast asleep, is Matter; Matter, when it is fully awakened, is Spirit.

Sri Chinmoy: I believe in evolution. We started from the mineral world and then evolved to the plant world, the animal world and the human world. And still our journey is not over. One day we shall become divine beings. But even when we were in the mineral world, we were not composed entirely of matter. Inside matter there is also spirit. Through our prayers and meditations we can bring forth spirit from matter and transform matter into spirit.

Question: What is the difference between astrology and Yoga?

Sri Chinmoy: Astrology does not have the power to change our fate, but spirituality or Yoga does have this power.

The difference between astrology and Yoga is that astrology only indicates; it indicates the future on the basis of the past, but it does not change it. Yoga, however, can actually defeat the past and shape the future.

Astrology plays its role most effectively until one has entered into deeper spirituality. There astrology bows down, as you bow down to me. Before one accepts spirituality, astrology is very powerful, like a lion. Then when one enters into a deeper spiritual life, astrology becomes a tiny household cat.

A heart of purity
Is indeed a citadel.
No undivine force
Can dare to challenge it.

CHAPTER ELEVEN

Meditation

Meditation is silence,
energising and fulfilling.
Silence is
the eloquent expression
of the inexpressible.

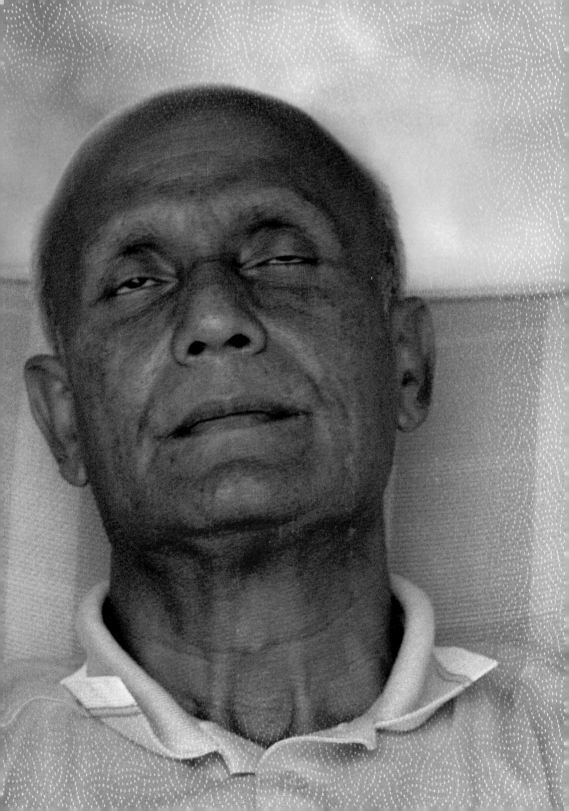

The essentials of meditation

Meditation is not an escape. Meditation is the acceptance of life in its totality, with a view to transforming it for the highest manifestation of the divine Truth here on earth.

Meditation is absolutely necessary for those who want to have a better and more fulfilling life. If you feel that you are satisfied with what you have and what you are, then you need not enter into the field of meditation. But if you feel that there is a barren desert deep inside your heart, then I wish to say that meditation is the answer. Meditation will give you inner joy and peace of mind. Meditation will never take you away from your parents, from your children, from your family. Far from it. Only it will strengthen your connection with your dear ones, because inside them you will see the very existence of God.

Meditation is not an escape. Meditation is the acceptance of life in its totality, with a view to transforming it for the highest manifestation of the divine Truth here on earth.

If you wish to develop your talents or increase your capacity in any field, then I wish to say that it is obligatory to follow some inner discipline. If you are a singer but you wish to sing infinitely better, if you aspire, I tell you, your voice will become far better. There is nothing on earth that cannot be improved through spirituality and meditation.

If you want to simplify your life, meditation is the answer. If you want to fulfil your life, meditation is the answer. If you want to have joy and offer joy to the world at large, then meditation is the only answer.

If you meditate to forget your suffering or to forget your difficulties, then you are not meditating for the right reason. But if you are meditating only to please God and fulfil God in His own way, then your meditation is correct.

When God is pleased, and God is fulfilled in your meditation, then it is God's business to take away your sufferings and difficulties. But if you meditate to escape from the world or to challenge the world and stand against the world, then you are doing the wrong thing.

Meditation is your conscious capacity that you have to utilise every day and every second to enter into your highest divinity, where the finite is completely lost in the Infinite. The finite existence which you have and which you are, can easily be lost in the infinite and become totally one with the infinite if you meditate. This is what meditation is and what meditation can do for you.

Question: How are we supposed to meditate?

Sri Chinmoy: Meditation depends on the individual standard. If you are a beginner in the field of meditation, you will meditate in one way and if you are advanced, naturally you will meditate in a different way. It depends on the individual standard, on the progress you have made.

For a beginner it is better to start with concentration. Otherwise, the moment you start meditating, millions of uncomely thoughts will enter into your mind. You will not be able to meditate for one second, whereas if you concentrate, you challenge the wrong thoughts entering into you.

Concentration gives us the capacity of intensity, and meditation gives us the capacity of vastness and sublimity. If you feel that you are to some extent advanced, then without concentration you can enter into meditation. Try to make your mind calm, quiet and vacant. Allow no thought into your mind, and then feel you are an express train which is constantly running and running, not stopping at any station. In meditation, try to feel you are a train running very fast towards your destination, and your goal is constantly transcending its own limit. Each time the train reaches the so-called goal, feel that it is only the starting point for your further goal. This is meditation. But for the beginner, instead of meditation, it is advisable to start with concentration.

Concentration, meditation, contemplation

When we want to develop will power, we concentrate. The mind is restless; constantly it moves from one idea to another. It cannot think of one thing for more than a fleeting minute. In concentration we focus only on one particular object or subject. We do not allow anything else to enter into our mind. If we know how to focus our concentration on a particular spot or on one of our chakras, we can concentrate on this. Through concentration we will be able to throw aside the many uncomely thoughts and undivine ideas that are in the mind.

Concentration acts like an arrow in the spiritual life. If doubt enters into our mind, the power of concentration will tear doubt to pieces. If fear enters into our mind, the power of concentration will chase away our fear. Concentration clears the way so that the traveller can walk along the path of meditation. How can we develop the power of concentration? We can develop concentration by leading a disciplined life, a pure life.

When we have become successful in concentration, we enter into the domain of meditation. When we meditate, we enter into the vast sea, the vast sky, and the reality of that vastness enters into our meditation. In meditation we see the whole sea all at once, whereas in concentration we take it drop by drop.

In contemplation we again go one step further. In contemplation we enter into the reality and the reality becomes part and parcel of our life.

Question: How often should we meditate?

Sri Chinmoy: You can meditate early in the morning and, if it is possible, in the evening before you go to bed. During the day, if you are free, and if you really get inspiration, then also you can meditate. But it is better to meditate well once a day in the morning, and to leave it for the rest of the day, than to sit five or six times a day with your eyes closed and just have pleasant thoughts drifting through your head.

Some people meditate three times, four times, six times a day. But I wish to say the number is of no consequence. If you feel really inspired, meditate twenty times. But if you do not feel any inspiration, then you are wasting your precious time and just deceiving yourself. Each time you meditate you have to offer your heart's breath and your soul's light that you are bringing to the fore. Only then is it worth meditating. Otherwise, you are just insulting your soul's possibilities. Please feel the necessity of meditating, even if it is for only one minute once a day. If it is done wholeheartedly, even if it is for a fleeting minute, then it is worthwhile. If inspiration is there, then meditate. That means that you have got the sanction from the Supreme. If it is the call of the Supreme, then you shall run fast, very fast, because He is the leader inside you.

> *Please feel the necessity of meditating, even if it is for only one minute once a day.*

Many people say that they meditate four times or six times a day. But what do they meditate on? They meditate on their bosses or they meditate on their boyfriends or their girlfriends. This is no meditation at all. If you can meditate most soulfully, if you feel that your aspiration is carrying you, only then is it really worthwhile meditation. But a day will come when your inner being will compel you to meditate twenty-four hours a day.

Question: What is the best time of day for my daily meditations, and what is the best length of time for these meditations?

Sri Chinmoy: The best time for meditation is early in the morning. When you get up, that is the best time. If you get up at 5:30, that is the best time. If you get up at 6:00, that is the best time. If you get up at 9:00, that too will be the best time, but you have to know that at that hour you will be swimming against the current. By that time the world has become full of noise and activities; everything is hustle and bustle. But if you get up at 5:00 or 6:00 or

7:00, you will still feel poise and peace in the atmosphere. So the earlier you can get up, the better.

Now, the length of time depends on your capacity. If you can meditate well for fifteen minutes, then do so. But if you just sit at your shrine for two hours, although your mind begins roaming after ten minutes, that is of no use. As long as you can meditate soulfully, you should meditate. But if you are just dragging it out and watching the clock to see how many hours you have meditated, that is of no use. If you can meditate well for fifteen minutes in the morning, that is more than enough.

Question: Usually after six-thirty I get the feeling that my meditation is over and I don't know what to do next. Should I just go back to sleep?

Sri Chinmoy: You can read spiritual writings, chant, or learn spiritual songs. Singing is also a form of meditation. Nobody is going to laugh at your voice when you are alone at home. There will be only you and the Supreme to observe. You can also do japa, repeating 'AUM' or 'Supreme' or your own spiritual name. If you read spiritual writings, sing spiritual songs and do japa, that is an extension of your meditation. But do not go back to sleep unless it is absolutely necessary for your health.

Question: How can we find our Inner Pilot and listen to it?

Sri Chinmoy: In order to find the Inner Pilot, you have to go deep within. Meditation is bound to carry you to the Inner Pilot. Meditation is a process that shows you how to go deep within. Meditation is a road that leads you to the ultimate destination. Meditation also is an inner assurance of your connection with the Absolute. When a seeker meditates, he hears the messages from Above, from his Beloved Father, or he hears messages from his own inner being. And when he tries to listen to the dictates of his inner being or the messages from Above, he transforms his outer life of imperfection into a life of perfect perfection.

In school you have a teacher who is teaching you and offering his wisdom-light to you through language. In the spiritual life also, the teacher teaches through language. But the language of the spiritual teacher is meditation. Meditation is the inner language, and the teacher teaches meditation through silence. It would not be easy for your professor to teach through silence, and for the student also it would not be easy to learn through silence. But a spiritual teacher will meditate for five minutes in silence and during his meditation he will offer peace, light and bliss. He can instruct you to meditate either by giving you specific instructions or through his silent gaze. But most of the time the spiritual teacher teaches through silence, because that way is most effective.

In school you are studying philosophy and you are using the searching mind. But in meditation, the mind is not used at all. That does not mean we have become an imbecile; far from it. Only you go far beyond the domain of the mind and in the realm of the soul you grow.

Question: Is a Master mandatory for proper meditation?

Sri Chinmoy: No one is forcing you to have a Master, but it certainly is advisable. You know that there is a goal, and you want to reach the goal. If you are wise, you accept help from someone who can show you the easiest, safest, and most effective path to that goal.

If you want to take hundreds and thousands of years to realise God, a spiritual Master is not necessary. But if you want to reach the Goal the fastest way, then certainly he is a necessity.

If you want to become a doctor, you go to school and study with doctors. If you do not study with a doctor, you will not operate on someone, because there you are dealing with human life. The Guru is like a spiritual doctor. He will operate on

> *If you want to take hundreds and thousands of years to realise God, a spiritual Master is not necessary.*

91

your fear, doubt and jealousy. First you doubt the existence of the Vast, the Unknown. Then you are afraid of the Vast because you feel that it is not a part of you and that it will engulf you. And then you are jealous of the Vast, because you feel that it is all illumination, fulfilment and perfection, whereas your life is all obscurity, frustration and imperfection. So before you can operate on others, first you have to study with a spiritual doctor, the spiritual Master. He will cure you and then teach you how to cure others.

Question: How do people meditate on your path?

Sri Chinmoy: Ours is the path of the heart. I tell my disciples that they have to empty their hearts totally so that Peace, Light and Bliss can descend from above and fill their inner vessel. If someone wants to follow the path of the heart, then all his emotional difficulties, worries, anxieties and undivine qualities will leave him and Peace, Light and Bliss from above will replace them.

So, when you meditate, you try to open the heart and the entire being. Sometimes you open the heart and keep the door open, and when the guest is about to enter, at that time you close the door. The amount of Peace, Light and Bliss that the inner vessel receives is measured. The vessel has its own consciousness. You may leave the vessel empty, but also it has to aspire to receive. Only then can you really have a good meditation.

Our progress will be faster if we meditate on the heart. When we meditate on the mind or inside the mind, we feel that already we know so much about the spiritual life. But when we go deep within, we come to learn that we know next to nothing about the spiritual life. Only we have gathered earthly information in our minds — information and nothing else. But when we meditate on the heart, we feel that we are like children who really want to learn everything fresh from the mother or from the father. The child feels that he does not know anything, but he wants to learn everything in a proper way.

So my advice for the seekers who would like to follow our path is to concentrate and meditate on the heart. And even those who will not fit in with our path can try to meditate on the heart. It is not only our path which emphasises the importance of meditating on the heart. There are other paths and other spiritual Masters who also advocate the same idea.

Question: Would you please be a little more specific when you say "meditate on the heart"? Do you mean to meditate on the physical heart or on the spiritual centre?

Sri Chinmoy: If you find it difficult to meditate on the spiritual heart, you can concentrate on the physical heart in the chest. But after you meditate there for a few months or for a year then you will feel that inside the ordinary human heart is the divine heart. And inside the divine heart is the soul.

Inside the divine heart is light, but inside the human heart, we can see the operation of the emotional vital. The emotional vital is located around the navel. But from there it can come into the physical heart and ruin everything by creating attachment. If one can meditate on the spiritual heart, there can be no attachment. It is all detachment. So we start with the human heart, and from the human heart we have to enter into the divine heart. Otherwise, if we remain with the human heart, we will quite often become a victim to attachment and emotional problems.

What is the first and foremost thing we expect from meditation? Peace. Peace and nothing else. Meditation is the embodiment of peace. The present-day world needs only one thing: peace.

Meditation techniques

The most important thing is practice. Today your mind acts like a monkey. This restless mind is knocking all the time at your heart's door and disturbing the poise of the heart. In this world everybody has pride, vanity and self-esteem. So if you keep your heart's door closed each time the mind comes, if you do not pay any attention to the mind, then after some time the mind will find it beneath its dignity to bother you.

Breathing slowly

Try to breathe in as slowly and as quietly as possible, so that if you place a tiny thread right in front of your nose it will not even move. Then you will see that your meditation is going to be deep and your mind will be very calm and quiet.

Imagining something vast

Imagine something very vast, and calm and quiet. When you start meditating, feel that inside you is a vast ocean and that you have dived deep within. There at the bottom it is all tranquility, tranquility's flood.

Breathing the cosmic energy

Feel that you are breathing in not just air but cosmic energy. Feel that tremendous cosmic energy is entering into you with each breath and that you are going to use it to purify your body, vital, mind and heart. Feel that there is not a single place in your body that is not being occupied by the flow of cosmic energy. It is flowing like a river inside you, washing and purifying your whole being.

Then, when you start to breathe out, feel that you are breathing out all the rubbish inside you — all your undivine thoughts, obscure ideas and impure actions. Anything inside your system that you call undivine, anything that you do not want to claim as your own, feel that you are exhaling.

Feeling a stream of love

When you are breathing in, feel a stream of divine love flowing in and through your body. You love yourself, you love God, you love your dearest and nearest ones, and you love humanity as a whole. So first please try to bring to the fore God's love aspect.

Love is the pioneer of all divine qualities. So when you cry for God, feel love — immediate, spontaneous, unreserved, soulful love.

One-four-two breathing

We have a traditional system of controlled breathing in India which is called *pranayama*, control of the life-breath. *Prana* is the vital energy, the life-breath; *yama* means control. The very first exercise you can practice is to repeat once, as you breathe in, the Name of God, the Christ or whomever you adore. Or, if your Master has given you a mantra, you can repeat that. This breath does not have to be long or deep.

Then hold your breath and repeat the same name four times. And when you breathe out, repeat two times the name or mantra that you have chosen. You inhale for one count, hold your breath for four counts, and exhale for two counts, inwardly repeating the sacred name. If you simply count the numbers — one-four-two — you do not get any vibration or inner feeling. But when you say the Name of God, immediately God's divine qualities enter into you. Then, when you hold your breath, these divine qualities rotate inside you, entering into all your impurities, obscurities, imperfections and limitations. And when you breathe out, these same divine qualities carry away all your undivine, unprogressive and destructive qualities.

> Love is the pioneer of all divine qualities. So when you cry for God, feel love—immediate, spontaneous, unreserved, soulful love.

95

The beginner starts with a one-four-two count. When he becomes mature in his breathing, he will be able to do it to a count of four-sixteen-eight: breathing in for four counts, holding the breath for sixteen, and breathing out for eight. But this has to be done very gradually. Some people even do this with an eight-thirty-two-sixteen count, but this is not for the beginner.

Meditating on a spiritual Master

When you want to practise concentration, you should choose something that gives you immediate joy. If you have a Master, your Master's picture will give you immediate joy. If you do not have a Master, select something that is very beautiful, divine and pure, like a flower, for example.

Chanting a mantra

Certain spiritual words are surcharged with a meaning or a condition or a consciousness that has developed in them from thousands of years of a special spiritual usage. When we enter deep into the significance of such a word, and reveal the very breath of the word and manifest its inner urge on the outer level, then the word fulfils its purpose, both inwardly and outwardly.

A mantra is an incantation. It can be a syllable, word, a few words or a sentence. When you repeat a mantra many times, it is called japa. A mantra represents a particular aspect of God, and each mantra has a special significance and inner power.

If you cannot enter into your deepest meditation because your mind is restless, this is an opportunity to utilize a mantra. You can repeat 'Supreme' or *Aum* or 'God' for a few minutes.

The sound of *Aum* is unique. Generally we hear a sound when two things are struck together. But *Aum* needs no such action. It is *anahata,* or unstruck; it is the soundless sound. A Yogi or spiritual Master can hear *Aum* self-generated in the recesses of his heart.

There are many ways to chant *Aum*. When you chant it loudly, you feel the omnipotence of the Supreme. When you chant it softly, you feel the delight of the Supreme. When you chant it silently, you feel the peace of the Supreme.

It is best to chant *Aum* out loud, so its sound can vibrate even in your physical ears and permeate your entire body. This will convince your outer mind and give you a greater sense of joy and achievement. When chanting out loud, the 'M' sound should last at least three times as long as the 'AU' sound.

Music and meditation

Meditation and music cannot be separated. When we cry from the inmost recesses of our heart for Peace, Light and Bliss, that is the best type of meditation. We cannot meditate twenty-four hours a day, but we can meditate, say, for two hours a day. Then we can play music or we can listen to music for a couple of hours a day. Next to meditation is music. But it has to be soulful music, the music that stirs and elevates our aspiring consciousness. When we play soulful music, psychic music, then immediately we are transported to the highest realm of consciousness. When we play music soulfully, we go high, higher, highest.

On the following page, you will find a selection of Sri Chinmoy's mantric English and Bengali songs.

O make my mind tranquil

Words and Music by
Sri Chinmoy
September 8, 1996

O make my mind tran - - - - -quil and calm.

Chā - ri- -di- ke ne- hā - ri- te_____ pră - shān - - - ti dhām

My own gratitude heart

♩ = 126 Moderate

November 1987

My own gra - ti - tude - - heart_____

is all that mat - - - - - ters.

Usha bala elo

Words and Music
By Sri Chinmoy
Fall 1977

♩.= 63 Moderate-slow

U - shā bā- - lā e - - lo (o)_____

dhi - re ā- - -ji dhi - re hri - dā - yā gā - bhi - re

(e)_____

Slowly, very slowly, the virgin dawn appears
In the very depths of my aspiration-heart.

Prayer and meditation

There is only one thing that we need here on earth and that is peace.
Everything else is meaningless and useless. We can get name, fame,
prosperity and everything on the outer plane. But if we do not find peace in
the inmost recesses of our heart, then we will never be satisfied. Only peace
can give us satisfaction. To find this
peace we have to dive deep within and
pray and meditate.

While you are praying, you are talking to
God and God is listening to you. While
you are meditating, God is talking and
you are listening.

> *Pray and meditate*
> *In any way you want,*
> *But your prayers*
> *and meditations*
> *Must be totally sincere.*

While you are praying, your prayer is going up high, higher, highest. Then
while you are meditating, God's Love, Light, Peace and Bliss are entering into
you. That is the difference between prayer and meditation.

There is also another difference. When you pray, try to feel that you are
utterly helpless. You have to pray like a beggar woman asking for alms:
"God, give me this." And you have to sincerely feel that you are in desperate
need of what you are praying for. You have to feel that your whole world
will collapse if you do not get it. Unless your prayer is fulfilled, you will be
absolutely hopeless.

When you meditate, on the other hand, you have to feel that you are the
dearest daughter* of God, with infinite wealth inside your heart. When
you meditate you are bringing to the fore your own divinity and inner
wealth — your own inner peace, inner bliss, inner love, inner joy. You are
not inventing these things; they belong to you and you are discovering them.

For those who want to realise the Highest, I always say that meditation
is of paramount importance. But there have been saints in the West who

---

* *This passage has been excerpted from Sri Chinmoy's answer to a female questioner.*

have realised God through prayer only. They did not know the concept of meditation. But the intensity of their prayers and their aspiration carried them into the world of meditation and beyond. Both approaches are effective. When we pray, we go up to God; when we meditate, God comes down to us. Ultimately the result can be the same.

The highest prayer is, "Let Thy Will be done." This is absolutely the highest reach of prayer, and it is also the beginning of meditation. Where prayer stops its journey, meditation begins. In meditation we say nothing, we think nothing, we want nothing. In the meditation-world the Supreme is acting in and through us for His own fulfilment. The prayer-world is always asking for something. But the meditation-world says, "God is not blind or deaf. He knows what He has to do to fulfil Himself in and through me. So I shall just grow into the Highest in soulful silence."

Be simple, be sincere,
Be pure and be humble.
Go back, go back once more
To the basics of your inner life.

Basics of the spiritual life

Simplicity

Simplicity is the soul, and the soul is the direct representative of God. For a few minutes, let us feel that we do not have a body, a vital, a mind or even a heart. What we have now and what we are is the soul alone, the direct representative of God. Please try to feel that you have become the soul. Do not give any form to this idea. Just repeat in silence, "soul, soul, soul," and feel that you have become a conscious and direct representative of God.

Sincerity

We all know what sincerity is. In the outer world, telling the truth is the highest form of sincerity. In the inner world, sincerity is seeing the Truth through God's Eye, feeling the Truth through God's Heart and growing into the Truth of God's transcendental Vision and universal Reality. This is inner sincerity. Now let us feel that we have grown into inner sincerity and that we are seeing everything through God's Vision, feeling everything through God's Heart and growing into God's transcendental Vision and universal Reality. Let us become inner sincerity.

Humility

There are many roads that lead to God-realisation, to the ultimate Truth; but the path of humility is the short-cut. We start on the road of our desire-life. That is the longest road. Then we become half spiritual: half desire and half aspiration. This road is not as long as the road of desire alone. The next road is the road of aspiration only. That road is a very short one, and humility will shorten it still more.

In the inner world, humility always reminds us of what we were previously, of what we are now and of what we are going to become. It was by virtue of our humility that we accepted the spiritual life. Humility is also eager to complete the game.

Each individual has two realities: the higher and the lower. The lower cherishes a sense of separateness from the higher, whereas the higher feels that without the lower it is incomplete. But it is the lower that has to grow into the higher. When we want to grow into the higher reality, we immediately see how far away we are. But if we are really humble in the inner world, then we make immediate progress. Then, when we dive deep within, we see how far we were six months ago and how much nearer we now are to divinity. We also see how different we are from our friends of the past. We are not criticizing them; but we see that our friends have not cultivated the inner cry to grow into divinity, into a higher consciousness.

It is humility that cultivates within us the eagerness to know and to grow into our higher reality. Everything is within us. But just because we are humble, the higher reality gets the opportunity to fulfill itself through us. The moment we lose our humility, we feel that we have nothing worth showing, that we have nothing that can be of any use to God. Let us meditate on our sincere inner humility for a few minutes.

Purity

In a broad sense, physical purity is cleanliness, vital purity is an open heart and mental purity is the absence of undivine or unhealthy thoughts. But if we really want to know what purity is, our gratitude-heart can tell us what it is. In the inner world, gratitude is the only purity. It is through gratitude, constant gratitude to the Supreme in us, that we expand our consciousness and come to know our higher vision and reality. If we can sow the seed of gratitude, it will germinate and grow into a tiny plant and then into a giant banyan tree. Then, under this huge banyan tree, in our gratitude-heart thousands of seekers will be able to take shelter and grow into their own divinity.

Our gratitude-heart is the pioneer-seeker, the path-finder, the God-server. For a few minutes, let us feel that what we are and eternally will become is nothing but a gratitude-heart.

Are we meditating well?

We can easily know whether we are meditating well or not just by the way we feel and see and think. Right after our meditation, if we have a good feeling for the world, then we know our meditation was good. If we see the world in a loving way in spite of its imperfections, if we can love the world even while seeing its teeming imperfections, our meditation was good. And if we have a dynamic feeling right after meditation, if we feel that we came into the world to do something, to become something, this indicates that we have done a good meditation. This feeling that we have to do something does not mean that we are feeding our human ambition. No! The moment we try to feed our ambition, it will entangle us like a serpent. What we have come into the world to do is what God wants us to do. What we have come into the world to become is what God wants us to become. What God wants us to do is to grow into His very image. What God wants us to become is His dedicated instrument. During our meditation if we get the feeling that God wants us to grow into His very image, wants us to be His dedicated instrument, and if this feeling is translated into action after our meditation, then we can be sure that we were meditating well.

If we can love the world even while seeing its teeming imperfections, our meditation was good.

But the easiest way to know if we have had a good meditation is to feel whether peace, light, love and delight are coming to the fore from within. Each time light comes forward, or love comes forward, or peace or delight comes forward, the whole body will be surcharged with that divine quality. When we have this experience we know that we have done a very good meditation. Each time divine qualities come to the fore, we are bound to feel that we are remembering a forgotten story. It is only through meditation that we can remember our forgotten story. This story was written by the seeker himself, by the seeker in us. The story was not written by somebody else. It is our own creation, but we have forgotten it, and it is meditation that brings it back. When we remember this story we are overjoyed that we have created such a beautiful story and that this is our life story.

Question: Is there any difference between meditation and self-hypnosis?

Sri Chinmoy: Yes. When we meditate, we become a perfect channel through which the Reality above us can flow. Here we surrender entirely to God's Will. "Let Thy Will be done": This is the acme of meditation. We bring down God's boundless Peace, Light and Bliss on the strength of our soulful meditation, and this Peace, Light and Bliss operates in and through us according to our capacity of receptivity.

But when we enter into the realm of self-hypnosis, we try to impose on our subconscious plane certain ideas or even ideals. We convince ourselves this is what has happened or this is what is going to happen. We try to bring to the fore, either from the subconscious world or from the inconscient world proper, thoughts which are not predominant or which have not yet come to the fore. We unconsciously or subconsciously bring up these ideas and make ourselves feel that these are realities which we once upon a time lived or which we are going to live in the near or distant future. So in the subconscious mind, formulated ideas or ideals operate.

But when we soulfully meditate, we go far beyond the realm of the thought-world. Here nature's Dance comes to an end. All thought-waves cease and we see reality in its pristine form.

Question: If you belong to a specific religious group, is it contradictory to meditate? Does meditation have one specific religion, or can anyone of any religion meditate?

Sri Chinmoy: Meditation far surpasses the barriers of religion. One can follow any religion. Meditation is like a school, and religion is like a house. You can go to a school or college no matter which house you live in. Everybody can meditate no matter what religion he belongs to or even if he does not belong to any religion.

Question: Can we use meditation to increase our creativity?

Sri Chinmoy: Certainly! Prayer and meditation are the only way. Many people are not born poets or born artists. But by practising meditation, they bring into their system literary capacities, painting capacities, musical capacities, because meditation means new life. When new life enters into you, you become a new man.

Before, you were not an artist, let us say. God gave you a particular type of life, with particular capacities. But when a new life enters into you, that means a new opportunity, a new avenue, a new light enters. At that time you can easily acquire the capacity of art.

One form of artistic capacity is to be able to draw something or play some instrument. But life itself can also be an art. How sincere one is to oneself, how sincere one is to God, how devoted one is to Truth — that is also an art. That particular art is not denied to anybody. That art, which is the supreme art, everybody can have. The other kinds of art are like branches which branch out from the art that is the life-tree. If one particular branch has most delicious fruits or beautiful flowers, naturally it adds to the beauty and wealth of the tree itself.

> *The best definition of prayer is to practice it daily.*
> *The best definition of meditation is to experience it soulfully.*
> *The best definition of yoga is to live it sincerely.*
> *The best definition of God is to love Him, and Him only, unconditionally.*

CHAPTER TWELVE

Food, health and fitness

We came into the world, not only to eat material food, but also to feed our heart with our aspiration-meal.

The role of diet

The vegetarian diet plays a most important role in the spiritual life. Purity is of paramount importance for an aspirant. This purity we must establish in the physical, the vital and the mental. When we eat meat and fish, the aggressive, animal consciousness enters into us. Our nerves become agitated; they become restless and aggressive, and this can interfere with our meditation. But the mild qualities of fruits and vegetables, on the other hand, help us to establish, in our inner life as well as in our outer life, the qualities of sweetness, softness, simplicity and purity. So, if we are vegetarians, it helps our inner being to strengthen its own existence. Inwardly, we are praying and meditating; outwardly, the food we are taking from Mother Earth is helping us too, giving us not only energy but also aspiration.

Question: You are a vegetarian. Is being a vegetarian essential in the spiritual life?

Sri Chinmoy: At the age of twelve I became a strict vegetarian. Being a vegetarian is not part of the tradition that I follow, and it is not essential for the spiritual life. However, I do feel that it can be of considerable help to us.

If we eat meat and fish, then the restless and aggressive qualities of the animal kingdom will enter into us. If our minds or other parts of our being are restless and aggressive, then we cannot have powerful and peaceful meditations. But if we eat only vegetables, then the mild qualities of the vegetable kingdom will enter into us and we will find it easier to have high and deep meditations. Therefore, being a vegetarian can be of considerable benefit to a seeker.

But I cannot say that if someone is not a strict vegetarian, he will not have high experiences or that God-realisation will always remain a far cry. No, it is not true. In the past there were great spiritual figures who ate meat and fish; even now there are spiritual figures who do so, and their lofty experiences and sublime realisations cannot be questioned. But I feel that it is good for people to adopt in their lives anything that can help them make fast, faster, fastest progress.

A vegetarian diet is of benefit to a sincere God-seeker, but it is not essential.

Question: What about eggs and milk and other dairy products?

Sri Chinmoy: Dairy products are fine. They do no harm because they do not have that kind of destructive vibration. But those who practise Kundalini Yoga and want to open the spiritual centres should not eat dairy products either. If one wants to open any of the six major centres, dairy products are harmful because they prevent the centres from opening. But if one wants the inner experience of Peace, Light and Bliss and does not care for the opening of the chakras, he can eat any dairy product.

Question: Does meditation require fasting or can we do it after eating?

Sri Chinmoy: If you want to have a deep meditation, a meditation of the highest order, you should not try to meditate just after eating a large meal. We have thousands of subtle nerves, spiritual nerves in our bodies. These nerves become heavy after a big meal and will not permit us to have the highest type of meditation. So it is always advisable to meditate on an empty stomach. If you want to have a most successful meditation, you should wait for at least an hour and a half or two hours after having a meal. But if you are really pinched with hunger when you go to meditate, your meditation will not be satisfactory. Your hunger, like a monkey, will constantly pinch you. You have to feed the monkey to quiet him for a few minutes. It is advisable at that time to have just a glass of milk or juice before meditating. This will not ruin your meditation.

And if you have meditated properly for half an hour or an hour, wait for at least fifteen minutes or a half hour before having a meal, because the result of the meditation should be assimilated before you enter into the world of food.

During that half hour, you can move around or read if you like. You may take a very small quantity of milk, soup or juice, but do not immediately eat a full meal. If you want to make a choice between meditation before the meal or after the meal, I always advise the seeker to meditate before the meal. Meditate for half an hour or so, then take fifteen minutes rest, and then eat. In that way the result of the meditation will be assimilated. But if you want to meditate after eating, even if you take an hour and a half rest, sometimes a lethargic consciousness will stand in the way of your highest meditation.

Fasting is not necessary for God-realisation... Fasting is not the answer. The answer is constant meditation.

Fasting, as you use the term, is not necessary for God-realisation. The Buddha tried that method. He adopted an austere life but found that it was of no use, so he embraced the middle path. By fasting we can purify ourselves to some extent. Once a week, or once a month, we can fast to purify our existence of outer aggressions and greed. But by fasting every day we approach death rather than God, who is all Life. Fasting is not the answer. The answer is constant meditation, soulful meditation, unreserved love for God and unconditional surrender to God.

Question: If one gets ill from food, is it usually because the cook was in a bad consciousness or is it really the quality of the food?

Sri Chinmoy: You can blame the bad consciousness of the cook, you can blame the quality of the food, and, again, you can blame your own bad consciousness. Sometimes the consciousness of the cook is very good and the consciousness of the food is very good, but the consciousness of the person who is eating is horrible. Therefore, he pays the penalty. True, sometimes the consciousness of the food is not praiseworthy or the consciousness of the cook is not praiseworthy, and therefore one may suffer from the food. But it also happens that the person who eats is in a very low consciousness. Then he will definitely suffer.

Question: How is it that some advanced people do not have to eat at all?

Sri Chinmoy: People who are spiritually advanced don't have to eat much if they don't want to. If they want to live on earth with very little food, then the Peace that they bring down from above will help them considerably. Their inner food can easily sustain them even if they eat very little material food. They can maintain themselves in this way if they want to. But if they want to remain on earth in a normal, natural way, eating material food, then they will take help from material food. It entirely depends on the individual choice.

Losing weight

You can meditate every day to lose weight. As soon as you start meditating, you have to think of yourself as a feather. You can keep a feather in front of you and feel that you are that feather. If your concentrative will-power is focused on that feather and if you can become one with the feather-consciousness, no matter what you eat, you will be able to lose weight. Your goal is not to become as light as a feather — far from it! The feather is only symbolic of lightness. If you can keep inside your mind a fixed idea that you are light, automatically the mind will put pressure on the physical. Imagination is a very strong power. Your imagination will be able to help you.

Imagination is a very strong power. Your imagination will be able to help you.

Question: Is there a spiritual way to break bad habits?

Sri Chinmoy: Certainly there is. Before you do anything always meditate for a minute or at least for a few seconds. The power of that meditation will enter into the bad habit like an arrow. Meditation, the soldier, will use his divine arrows against bad habits. This is absolutely the best way.

Healing and spirituality

Meditation includes everything. In meditation we enlarge our consciousness until it includes everything in the universe. There is nothing we cannot achieve through meditation.

Each individual has the capacity to heal if a person knows how to concentrate and meditate, and especially how to concentrate on physical ailments. There is no ailment in God's creation that he won't be able to cure. But we have to know if it is God's Will for us to heal someone. Otherwise, we may act like the hostile forces who want to break the rules of the divine Game.

Question: What do you think of healing in relation to spirituality?

Sri Chinmoy: I wish to say a few words from the spiritual point of view about what I think of healing. Healing deserves special attention and, at the same time, special appreciation from spirituality. An ordinary healer heals a person in order to get name or fame or just because he has an inner urge to help humanity. But a spiritual person heals a particular person only when God asks him to or when he gets personal permission from God to do so.

When an ordinary healer heals a person, he is often affected by the disease or the ailment of the patient. Very often I come across people who have healed and then themselves become victims of those ailments that they have cured in some other people. Some actually die of the disease they have cured in others. But when a spiritual person cures someone, he cures with his soul's light. He enters into the sufferer with his soul's light, and he cures the person without becoming attached. There is a continuous cosmic flow in and through his life, and that continuous flow of cosmic energy enters into the patient from him. Then it is just as though light were permeating the entire body of the person who is suffering. So a spiritual person heals only when he is commanded by the Divine or when he gets special permission from the Divine. Then he becomes totally one with the sufferer on the strength of his soul's oneness, and cures with his light.

Mantra for improved health

If you are physically weak, if your physical constitution is not satisfactory, you can chant sincerely and soulfully:

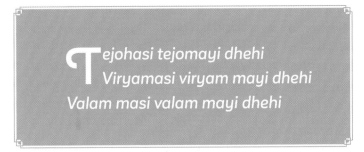

Tejohasi tejomayi dhehi
Viryamasi viryam mayi dhehi
Valam masi valam mayi dhehi

In a week's time you will see a change for the better in your health. It means:

I pray for dynamic energy;
I pray for dynamic virility;
I pray for indomitable physical strength.

Sport and physical fitness

Physical fitness is of great importance in our life. If the body is in good condition, then we can perform all our life-activities well. So it is important to run or do physical exercises every day in order to become strong, healthy and dynamic. If we are physically fit, we will be able to keep ailments and other uninvited guests from entering into us.

In the absolutely ancient tradition, in Vedic times and in the time of the Mahabharata, they practiced archery and all sorts of things; they were physically strong. Then came an era for lethargy-prone people, so they separated spirituality very nicely from the physical, the vital and the mind. They created a big gap between the two and said, "If you are spiritual, you cannot do physical things, and if you are physically active, you cannot pray and meditate." But we say, "No, spirituality can be in the physical and the physical can be in the spiritual." This is our philosophy.

You are praying in the morning and then you are going out running. So everything you are doing together. This moment you are taking a step with your left leg; the next moment, with your right leg. Outer running you are doing and inner running you are doing. Inwardly you are concentrating and outwardly you are taking exercise. So for you, the body and the soul are going together.

If we are physically fit, then we will be more inspired to get up early in the morning to meditate.

The body is like a temple and the soul or inner reality is like the shrine inside the body-temple. If the temple does not have a shrine, then we cannot appreciate the temple. Again, if we do not keep the temple in good condition, then how can we take proper care of the shrine? We have to keep the body fit, and for this, running is of considerable help. If we are physically fit, then we will be more inspired to get up early in the morning to meditate.

True, the inspiration to meditate comes from within, but if we are healthy, then it will be much easier for us to get up at five or six o'clock to pray and meditate. In this way the inner life is being helped by the outer life. Again, if we are inspired to get up early to meditate, then we will also be able to go out and run. Here we see that the outer life is being helped by the inner life.

Both outer running and inner running are important. A marathon is twenty-six miles. Let us say that twenty-six miles is our ultimate goal. When we first take up running, we cannot run that distance. But by practising every day we develop more stamina, speed and perseverance. Gradually we transcend our limited capacity, and eventually we reach our goal. In the inner life our prayer and meditation is our inner running. If we pray and meditate every day, we increase our inner capacity.

The body's capacity and the soul's capacity, the body's speed and the soul's speed, go together. The outer running reminds us of something higher and deeper — the soul — which is running along Eternity's Road. Running and physical fitness help us both in our inner life of aspiration and in our outer life of activity.

The body needs proper training so that it will be fit to receive the message of the soul. If the body is strong and healthy, it can receive the message of the soul unreservedly, and we can become a perfect receptacle, a perfect instrument. At that time the soul's aspiration and the body's aspiration go together.

So please exercise regularly. Your strong body will someday be necessary for the manifestation of the Supreme. The higher, the deeper you go, the more it will be necessary for you to reveal and manifest your inner divinity; and for that manifestation, physical fitness is of paramount importance.

CHAPTER THIRTEEN

Family life

The sacred and divine purpose of the family
is to help each individual member to discover
his own real reality.

The role of a family

Question: How much does our childhood influence us?

Sri Chinmoy: It depends on the family, it depends on the parents, it depends on the environment. If you come of a religious family, a spiritual family, then there is every possibility that this will be stamped on your forehead, or it will be written on the tablet of your heart. There is every possibility that the seed that was sown by your parents will germinate and become a huge tree with many flowers and fruits.

It all depends on the individual. There are many people who have received tremendous, tremendous affection as children. Sometimes, at the very end of one's life, the parents' affection and compassion remains because they have influenced the person's life so much. Again, after fifteen or twenty years, some people do not care for their father's good qualities or their mother's good qualities. They want to stay on their own. Many children keep no connection with their parents. Everything depends on the individual — how much the individual wants to retain the affection, love, sweetness and fondness from his parents.

Question: What if your childhood experiences were not so nice?

Sri Chinmoy: If you feel that your parents were not nice, if you did not get good treatment from your parents right from your infancy, then you have to take your imagination as a reality. Imagine once again your childhood. You were brought up in one family, but right around you, in your vicinity, some parents were extremely, extremely nice to their children. Identify with them, identify, identify!

Always try identification. You did not receive love and affection, perhaps, but now you can definitely apply your imagination and imagine love and affection. Just think of one particular family where the parents were so indulgent to their children. That imagination will definitely give you sweetness, happiness and a feeling of inner fulfilment.

If your parents were not kind, just imagine sweetness, sweetness, sweetness. Early in the morning, look at a flower, look at the dawn. If you can identify yourself with nature, you are getting tremendous joy. At that time, are you thinking about how your parents struck you black and blue? You are the same person, but your wisdom has to work. You have to bring forward sweet memories, sweet memories, sweet memories. If you do not have sweet memories in your immediate family, that cannot prevent you from getting sweetness from your childhood.

Now that you are mature, you have to use wisdom at every moment. Exercise wisdom, wisdom, wisdom! Sometimes in a family, parents get angry. They stop their children when they want to go to university, or they do not pay the costs. In the end, if one accepts the spiritual life, it means one has to forgive them. It is very difficult sometimes, when we do not forgive a person, to bring sweetness out of our memories of that person.

If your parents were not nice, first forgive them. By harbouring bitter memories of your parents' so-called misconduct, you will never be able to bring your own inner sweetness to the fore. You have to forgive your parents and forget the sad experience. If absolute necessity demands, you may even have to forget about your parents. Only try to imagine yourself, with your consciousness as a seven-year-old, to see how children elsewhere were given tremendous affection, sweetness and fondness.

Question: Do you feel marriage is compatible with the spiritual life?

Sri Chinmoy: It is up to the individual to decide whether or not marriage is compatible with his or her spiritual life. It is not at all obligatory for a seeker to get married. It entirely depends on the individual. To say that marriage is compatible with the spiritual life is to say something which may be very far from the truth in some cases. It is the individual seeker who has to decide whether marriage and the spiritual life can and should go together for him or for her.

In a good marriage, immediately two eyes become four eyes, two arms become four arms. Everything is doubled: strength, consciousness, reality, divinity, everything. In a bad marriage, everything is weakened. Frustration looms large and, finally, destruction plays its role most ruthlessly. There is no hard and fast rule that one should not get married in the spiritual life or that one should get married. It entirely depends on the soul's decision.

Mutual faith, mutual love, mutual sacrifice and mutual self-giving are the ingredients for a successful spiritual marriage.

Most marriages are founded either on the need to assuage loneliness or on the need to fulfil the demands of the lower vital. Marriage may or may not be compatible with the spiritual life in any particular case. Some souls feel that through marriage they will be able to make faster progress, while others feel that marriage will be a hindrance to their spiritual progress. I often say that single people can run the fastest in the spiritual life. But God and the individual souls must make the decision, not the human mind.

We have to know what God wants. When we meditate, when we aspire, we come to learn God's Will. If it is God's Will, naturally there will be no difficulty in realising the truth after entering into married life. But, if it is not God's Will, then we have to be very careful. We are then, consciously or unconsciously, putting a heavy burden on our shoulders. Each individual has to decide if married life is necessary for him personally.

Question: Do you feel it is necessary for a couple to be legally married?

Sri Chinmoy: As long as human beings want to live in society, and as long as society has something to say about the welfare of the world, legal marriage is of utmost importance.

120

Question: What is the importance of the marriage ceremony and what is its inner meaning?

Sri Chinmoy: The outer importance of the marriage ceremony is to share joy with others — with dear ones and well-wishers. The inner importance is to convince the outer mind that here on earth, where division reigns supreme, oneness can also play its role.

Question: For what purpose is the union between man and woman?

Sri Chinmoy: When union takes place between a man and a woman, each one gives a significant or insignificant meaning to the action. But in the highest, deepest spiritual life, when the realisation of oneness with all humanity is coming to the fore, this ordinary human union does not serve any purpose. One can have physical relations with someone hundreds of times, but the real union, the inner union, does not take place. Only when we can establish our soul's union with a person will we be fulfilled. When we can liberate ourselves from the meshes of ignorance, and when we can realise the entire earth as our own, when we feel that all of mankind is our very own, then only can we have proper union. Physical union is no union in comparison to the all-pervading union of spiritual oneness which we can have.

I am telling you all this from the strict spiritual point of view. We have to reach a certain level before we can reject the ordinary human relation. Delight and pleasure are two different things. If one cares for the inner spiritual life, one will get delight. If one cares for the ordinary human life, one will get pleasure. Pleasure is bound to be followed by frustration because in pleasure there is no permanent fulfilment. But delight itself is all-fulfilling. This delight we get only in the spiritual union with the Divine, with our inner being. We have to know what we want. If we want pleasure, the union between man and woman is enough for a while. But if we want delight, which is the nectar of Immortality, which is immortal Bliss, then we have to launch into the path of spirituality and establish the supernal union between man and God.

Question : I've read in some places that the use of sexual energy means that you use up some spiritual energy at the same time. Is this true? In that case, what can be done if one wants to lead a spiritual life?

Sri Chinmoy: What you have read is absolutely true. The animal human life and divine God-life do not and cannot go together. But one cannot realise God overnight. It is impossible. You do not get your Master's degree in the twinkling of an eye, or in a day, or even in a year. It may require twenty years of study to achieve. God-realisation is also a study, the most difficult subject. It takes quite a few years. Fifteen, twenty, thirty years, even many lifetimes, many incarnations, are required to realise God.

One cannot realise God overnight. It is impossible.

But if you tell a beginner that he will have to give up all his lower vital life and everything of that sort all at once, he will say, "Impossible! How can I do that?" If he has to give up all his lower vital propensities the moment he enters into the spiritual life, he will never enter into the spiritual life at all. So instead, he has to make headway towards his Goal slowly and steadily. He should not try to give up everything all at once. It is just like smoking or drinking. If someone feels that drinking excessively is a serious obstacle to his spiritual life, let him try to minimise it slowly. If he is drinking five times a day, let him try to drink four times a day instead. Then, after a few months, let him try to make it three times a day. Then, after considerable time, he can make it twice. Gradually, slowly, if he tries to diminish his hankering after drinking, he will be successful. This way, it will not tell upon his health. Otherwise, it will only be a great struggle. The body will resist and it will break down.

So, in the spiritual life also, the lower vital nature, which you may call sex, has to be gradually conquered. If one enters into the spiritual life and says, "Today I shall conquer all my lower propensities," he is just fooling himself. Tomorrow his mind will be in doubt. His physical mind will torture him.

His impure and cruel vital will try to punish him in every way. He will feel miserable. He will be frustrated and inside his frustration will loom his own destruction.

Question: Do you feel that some kind of formal spiritual practice is of benefit to the harmony of marriage? If you do think so, what kind of practice would you recommend?

Sri Chinmoy: Yes, there should always be some spiritual practices. These spiritual practices alone will enable the seekers to have harmony in their marriage. Purity in thought and action, patience, both in the inner life and the outer life, and always to live in the loving heart rather than in the doubting mind — these are the spiritual practices that can support a marriage.

Question: Do you have any recommendations for dealing with quarrelling and misunderstanding in a spiritual marriage?

Sri Chinmoy: Constant prayer for peace of mind and for the soul to come to the fore, for the expansion of the heart's all-loving capacity, can alone solve all misunderstandings and quarrels.

Question: When do you feel divorce is the best course of action?

Sri Chinmoy: When everything else has failed. When the power of oneness has failed, when the power of love has failed, when the power of compromise has failed, when everything has failed in keeping two lives together, then divorce is the best action.

Divorce is detrimental when the inner beings want to continue to be together, when the inner beings feel that, in the course of time, both husband and wife will better understand each other and lead a more illumining life. The inner beings must determine whether or not the marriage should be continued. If the seekers do not listen to the voice of their inner beings, if their outer minds compel them to get a divorce, then the divorce will be detrimental to their spiritual progress. It is the inner beings that should determine both marriage and divorce.

Question: What is the mother's duty and father's in bringing up children?

Sri Chinmoy: The mother's duty is to teach the children how to pray, how to be simple, sincere and loving. These are a few things that the mother should take as her bounden duty in bringing up her children.

The best attitude for bringing up children is guidance, compassion, forgiveness and conscious oneness.

The father's responsibility is to teach his knowledge and wisdom and to bring to his children the message of the vast world. The little family is not all; there is a large family also. The mother will use all her loving, intimate, affectionate qualities. The father will also do that, but he will also bring the message of the outer world to the children. The mother will make the little family sweet, sweeter, sweetest, and the father will bring the outer world closer to the children. He will make them feel that there is another world which has to be housed inside the little world, or that the little world has to be part and parcel of that large world.

Question: What is the parents' responsibility for the formal education of their children?

Sri Chinmoy: The parents have to take full responsibility for the formal education of their children. They have to send the children to school. They have to give proper attention to their children's studies, to their outer behaviour and to their inner growth. Children must not be left alone. At every moment the parents should take considerable interest in the children's welfare. In the formative years, the parents must play a most significant

role. Children are like tiny saplings or plants. They have to be sheltered and taken proper care of by the parent until they have grown into large and strong trees.

Question: What advice can you offer to single parents?

Sri Chinmoy: To those who are single parents because of divorce, my only suggestion is that they should not speak ill of the other party to their children. The children should not be influenced. Let the children listen to the dictates of their own hearts. Let them feel that both their father and their mother are good. Let their hearts, like magnets, pull the good qualities of the father and of the mother. Neither the father nor the mother should consciously or unconsciously influence the children against the other partner.

Parents should be very careful if they get a divorce. They should pay extra attention to the children, for when the family breaks, the consciousness of the children will break automatically. And who is responsible? The parents are one hundred percent responsible; therefore, they should take action to rectify the situation as well as they can. They can only do so by giving their children more love, abundant love, and by showing the children that their separation will in no way affect their love for them. What is of paramount importance is love. They have to offer their children boundless love.

Question: What is the proper attitude towards money and possessions for householders?

Sri Chinmoy: Householders must take money as material power, which has to be utilised divinely. Money-power is not to be used to lord it over others, but to meet with the necessities of life. This power has to be used judiciously, devotedly and in a fulfilling manner. Money has considerable power, but whether it is good or bad depends on the individual. The individual can use it divinely or undivinely. When money-power is used properly, it is a divine boon; if it is misused, it is a veritable curse.

CHAPTER FOURTEEN

Meditation in the workplace

We can arrive
at perfection's gate
Only when we work together
Lovingly, untiringly
and selflessly.

Developing the inner capacity

It is possible to bring meditative consciousness into the work you do, but you have to know how far you have already walked along the path of spirituality. If you want to be a singer, you cannot become a good singer overnight. For a dancer also it takes time to learn to do the steps in perfect order. But eventually the dancer and the singer become experts. Then they can do many things at a time. When a doctor performs an operation, an ordinary person would be wonderstruck to see how many things he can concentrate on at once. When you are just learning to drive, you are nervous; but once you become an expert driver, you can look at this side and that side but everything is under perfect control.

How can we develop this kind of capacity? In the beginning, it is impossible. If somebody says he has entered into the spiritual life today and today he has this capacity, rest assured that he is fooling himself. But this capacity is like a muscle. When you take exercise, you develop your muscles. In the spiritual life also, if each day you practise meditation regularly, devotedly and soulfully, then you are bound to develop these inner capacities. Then, when you are in the office, when you are in school or when you are in some other place with your friends, you will feel an inner presence guiding you. Even if you talk about earthly, mundane things you will not lose the inner wealth that you have accumulated during your meditation.

In the beginning, perhaps the seeker starts with only five minutes of meditation early in the morning. Then a day comes when he can sit and meditate for half an hour, then an hour, then two hours; and he can meditate well more often, not just on rare occasions. Some people sit, but they are not meditating at all. But if somebody can meditate for two or three hours at a stretch with perfect equanimity, without losing his mental balance, naturally he has made some progress in his inner strength, inner power and inner light. Everything depends on one's achievement. Things he has really achieved in the spiritual life, he can use. If I have money, I can give it to you if I want to; but if I don't have money, in spite of my best intentions, I will not be able to give it to you. Inner power, inner light and all the divine qualities are inside you. Your inner being has accumulated them. Now these qualities have to be brought to the fore.

We have to go to work, we have to go to the office or to school. Your classes may not be spiritual at all. Others are trying to create problems; they are trying to influence you unconsciously or consciously. You become a victim to their merciless treatment, and then you are totally lost. But if your inner being supplies you with your own inner peace and joy, then you will be able to swallow their undivine behaviour. You will be answering your professor's questions or talking to your boss, but inside you will feel the presence of your own inner being which helped you when you were meditating early in the morning. You will feel its presence like a divine child within you.

Question: How can you maintain inner tranquillity at work when you are in an atmosphere with a great deal of pressure?

Sri Chinmoy: You can maintain inner tranquillity no matter what happens in your office or how many wrong forces from your office try to assail you, provided you feel that these forces are no match for your love of light. When you are in the office, you are constantly attacked by the force of doubt, which is a representative of darkness. If you feel that you have nothing with which to fight this force, then you are totally lost. But if you feel that inside your heart there is something called light, and that this boundless luminosity is infinitely more powerful than the force attacking you, then you have nothing to fear. Because you pray and meditate and are trying constantly to increase your love of God, and because you are aware of God's Presence inside your heart, you can rest assured that you definitely embody light.

The wrong forces are coming from outside. But inside you is the strongest, mightiest force, which is in constant communication with the Almighty Absolute. This force is your inner light, which is immortal. It will never surrender to the wrong forces. In fact, when darkness consciously or unconsciously enters into light, it is bound to be transformed. Just by bringing this inner light to the fore, you will see to your great astonishment that the outer darkness immediately will give way. The more you can increase your inner light and bring it to the fore through your prayer and meditation, the sooner you will see the transformation of the outer forces that are attacking you.

> *The more you can increase your inner light and bring it to the fore, the sooner you will see the transformation of the outer forces.*

Question: How can you overcome feelings of resentment and anger that you feel when your superiors appear to be unfair?

Sri Chinmoy: When we work in a group, there are many individuals, many ideas, many thoughts and propensities working together. But we have to do our best to feel that all the individuals in the group, all the ideas and propensities, are part and parcel of our own existence. We have to feel that they are all limbs of our own body, and that all our limbs are working together.

We feel that our superiors do not understand us, do not value us, do not appreciate our sincere effort and dedication. By arguing with our superiors, by trying our utmost to convince them that they are wrong or that they have no feeling of oneness and sympathy with us, we cannot change their way of life. But if we take them as part and parcel of our own existence and feel that we belong to them and that they belong to us, then we can change them.

If we consider our superiors as human beings who are totally different from us, who are perfect strangers to our ideals, ideas and goals, then we shall never be able to get happiness from life. We have to consider our superiors as limbs, or as branches of the one reality-tree. Then, if we notice that one branch is not functioning well, we try to cure that particular branch with our inner love, inner concern, inner light. If today our arms are defective, or if any part of our existence-reality is suffering from a particular shortcoming, what do we do? We focus all our concentration on the defective part and show it all our concern, love, sweetness and affection. We try to muster the rest of our being and show all concern to the defective part. And we eventually cure the defective part.

By a mere wishful attitude we cannot bring this about. In order to do this most effectively, we have to pray and meditate in silence to the Author of all good. It is He alone who has the capacity to cure a defective limb, and He is more than willing to listen to our prayer for the transformation of our so-called 'superiors'. So, it is only our inner prayer and meditation that can eventually and radically change their life. But before that happens, we can try to feel that they belong to us and we belong to them. We can feel that their misunderstanding, their lack of faith in us and lack of appreciation for what we do, is a fault, a defect, in our own existence-reality.

Question: While I am in the office, how can I control my emotions? There is so much injustice and nothing I can do to help myself.

Sri Chinmoy: Right now injustice is creating suffering in your life. Some people in your office are striking you inwardly, and because of your fear or incapacity you cannot protect yourself. But if you become very strong inwardly, you can use this strength either to take yourself to some other plane where their attacks will not reach you or to give them some illumination so they will stop bothering you.

Injustice is a kind of negative or undivine power, whereas light is a divine power. If you seriously enter into the spiritual life and learn how to invoke God's Light and Compassion, these divine forces will definitely save you from the situation that is now causing you suffering. But this may take a little time.

A quicker way of saving yourself is to acquire peace of mind. At our meditations here at the United Nations, we bring down peace. This peace is not something imaginary; it is very real. When you meditate with us, you can not only feel this peace but you can actually swim in the sea of peace. This peace is a solid power, which is infinitely more powerful than injustice. When you are swimming in the sea of peace, no human power can upset you.

Peace is the most effective weapon with which to conquer injustice.

Right now when these people attack you, you become angry and upset because you feel they are of the same standard as you. But when your whole being is flooded with peace, then no matter what other people do, you will feel that they are like children playing in front of you. You will say, "These are all children. What can I expect from them?"

When you have to defend yourself or protect yourself, always try to use a higher weapon. If people say something and you retaliate on their level, there will be no end to it. Again, if you simply swallow your anger, they will continue to take advantage of you. But if you are inundated with inner peace, they will see something in you that can never be conquered. They will see a change in you, and this change will not only puzzle them but also threaten and frighten them. It will make them realise that their weapons are useless.

Peace is the most effective weapon with which to conquer injustice. If you pray and meditate regularly, you will soon feel that your peace is infinitely stronger, more fulfilling and more energising than the unfortunate situations that others create.

Question: If I do not respect the person I am working with, I do not know how to behave.

Sri Chinmoy: There is something called practical wisdom. Suppose you see that your boss is completely wrong about something. If you fight with your boss and you are in his bad books, then he will eventually fire you. Nobody wants to be corrected or perfected. That is human life, especially in the case of bosses. It is beneath their dignity to be corrected by their subordinates.

Practical wisdom says that if your boss fires you, you will be in trouble. If your boss gives you a very bad report, then you will be in trouble. I am not saying you should flatter your boss. But at that point you can ignore the situation. You can say to yourself, "My boss is wrong. What am I going to do? If I try to perfect him or correct him, then he will get mad." So you can act as if you have not seen anything; you can be blind to the situation. That is called practical wisdom.

Question: How can we have oneness with our fellow workers?

Sri Chinmoy: If your fellow workers are not spiritual or spiritually inclined, then you have to exercise more compassion and sacrifice. If somebody needs more kindness and affection, then you should be ready to give it to that person — not according to what he deserves but according to your own heart's magnanimity. If somebody is nasty to you or is not helping you in your work, you have to take it as a challenge to become extra nice, extra kind and extra sweet so that you can bring forward the good qualities in that person. Some people are good, some are bad. If we treat bad ones the way they treat us, we will enter into the animal world. So we have to work in a divine way and try to conquer them through patience, concern and love.

Question: If you work for a company and are selling a product, you are trying to get material gain for the company. How do you reconcile that and put your energies into it?

Sri Chinmoy: The important thing you have to know is whether or not you are participating in deception. Suppose you are selling sugar for a company, and you know that they have mixed something into the sugar to deceive the customers. Then, if you really want to be spiritual, you must not work for this kind of company. But if you sell something for what you call profit, that is not deception. If you buy something for two dollars and sell it for two dollars, then how are you going to earn your livelihood? You have to sell it for two-fifty or three dollars. Profit is not deception. But how much profit? If you buy something for two dollars and sell it for twenty, then you are just exploiting people. During the war, people knew that the price of things would go very high, so they bought things for six dollars that should sell for twelve dollars at most. Then they were able to sell them for ninety dollars. Just because something was unavailable and people wanted it badly, this kind of exploitation was possible. So you have to know if you are deceiving or exploiting your customer, and you have to strike a balance between exploitation and stupidity.

Question: How can we aspire when we are working?

Sri Chinmoy: In the morning, when you pray and meditate, feel that you have gained real wealth in the form of peace, light and bliss. As you keep your money inside your wallet, so you can keep your peace, light and bliss inside your heart. Then, when ignorance comes, with your spiritual wealth you can threaten or conquer the undivine force that is approaching you. With money-power you can buy anything you want. Similarly, the spiritual power you get from prayer and meditation is a real power. When people are shouting, screaming and behaving undivinely, just bring forward the inner power which you have kept inside your heart. Think of how much peace, light and bliss you got early in the morning. Peace is power, light is power, bliss is power, just as money is power. Just bring it forward and you will not have any difficulty at all.

There is no such thing
As insignificant work.
Therefore, we must needs do everything
With our heart's love
And our life's respect.

ABOUT THE AUTHOR

Sri Chinmoy was born in the village of Shakpura in East Bengal, India (now Bangladesh) in 1931. He was the youngest of seven children in a devout family. In 1944, after the passing of both of his parents, he joined his brothers and sisters at the Sri Aurobindo Ashram, a spiritual community near Pondicherry in South India. He meditated for several hours a day, having many deep inner experiences. It was here that he first began writing poetry to convey his widening mystical vision. He also took an active part in ashram life and was a champion athlete for many years.

Heeding an inner command, Sri Chinmoy moved to the United States in 1964 to be of service to spiritual aspirants in the Western world. During the 43 years that he lived in the West he opened more than 100 meditation Centres worldwide and served as spiritual guide to thousands of students. Sri Chinmoy's boundless creativity found expression not only in poetry and other forms of literature, but also in musical composition and performance, art and sport. In each sphere he sought to convey the diverse experiences that comprise the spiritual journey: the search for truth and beauty, the struggle to transcend limitations, and the supremely fulfilling communion of the human soul with the Divine.

As a self-described student of peace who combined Eastern spirituality and Western dynamism in a remarkable way, Sri Chinmoy garnered international renown. In 1970 at the request of U Thant, the third Secretary-General of the United Nations, he began the twice-weekly peace meditations for delegates and staff members at UN headquarters that continued until the end of his life. Sri Chinmoy enjoyed a special friendship with many international luminaries including President Mikhail Gorbachev, Mother Teresa, President Nelson Mandela and Archbishop Desmond Tutu.

On 11 October 2007, Sri Chinmoy passed away. His creative, peace-loving and humanitarian endeavours are carried on worldwide by his students, who practise meditation and strive to serve the world in accordance with his timeless teachings.

For more information about Sri Chinmoy kindly visit *www.srichinmoy.org*

Learn to meditate with the Sri Chinmoy Centre

Sri Chinmoy Centres give meditation classes in over 350 cities all over the world. Sri Chinmoy asked his students to offer these classes to the general public free of charge, as he felt that the inner peace that meditation could bring was the birthright of each individual.

Find a meditation class near you on *www.srichinmoycentre.org*

Recommended books of Sri Chinmoy

222 Meditation Techniques

These 222 guided exercises, the largest collection of meditation techniques in one book, are suitable for both beginners and advanced seekers who wish to explore the world of meditation. From breathing exercises, guided meditations and the use of mantras, to special exercises for runners, artists and musicians, ways to overcome depression, stress and bad habits, and even losing weight, this book offers a truly broad canvas of possibilities.

www.themeditationbook.net

Sport & Meditation
The Inner Dimension of Sport

This is a unique book, which challenges our preconceptions of our physical capacities and of the limitations of age. It includes specific exercises concerning meditation, concentration and mantra as aids to the focus needed in all forms of exercise and training. It is this new facet that enables us to achieve peak performance, to get more from exercise and to enjoy robust and lasting health and wellbeing.

World champions such as Carl Lewis, Tatyana Lebedeva, Tegla Loroupe, Bill Pearl, and Paul Tergat share their own inner secrets and spiritual perspectives on training and competition in anecdotes peppered throughout the book.

www.sportandmeditation.com

Heart-Wisdom-Drops
Inspiring Aphorisms for Every Day

This collection of 55 inspirational cards makes an excellent gift. Each card features an aphorism and meditative painting by Sri Chinmoy. For those seeking hope, peace of mind and life-wisdom these cards offer inspiration, and are a guide to a happy, harmonious and spiritually-grounded daily life.

www.wisdom-cards.com

For more books kindly visit *www.srichinmoybooks.com*

Explanatory notes

(Excerpted from Sri Chinmoy's writings)

AUM

Aum is a syllable with a special significance and creative power. Aum is the mother of all mantras. When we chant AUM, what actually happens is that we bring down Peace and Light from above and create a universal harmony within and without us. When we repeat AUM, both our inner and our outer beings become inspired and surcharged with divine Light and aspiration. AUM has no equal. AUM has infinite Power. Just by repeating AUM, we can realise God.

Aspiration

Aspiration is an inner hunger for God's Love, Light and Bliss. Aspiration is inner cry. Cry, cry like a child from the very depths of your heart. There is no prayer that cannot be answered, no meditation that cannot be fulfilled if you cry sincerely. Aspiration is your soul's mounting cry to reach the Highest and to bring down the Highest into the earth's consciousness.

Chakras

There are three principal channels through which this life-energy flows. These channels meet together at six different places. Each meeting place forms a centre. Each centre is round like a wheel. Indian spiritual philosophy calls these centres chakras. All real spiritual Masters, from the very depth of their experience, say that it is better to open the heart centre first and then try to open the other centres.

Guru

Guru is a Sanskrit word which means 'he who illumines'. The one who offers illumination is called a Guru. According to my own inner realisation I wish to say that there is only one real Guru, and that is the Supreme. No human being is the real Guru. But although the Supreme alone is the real Guru, here on earth we value time. If we find someone who can help us on our journey towards illumination, we take his help, and we may call him our Guru.

Japa

Japa is the repetition of a mantra. AUM is a mantra; it is not japa. If you repeat AUM twice, thrice or hundreds of times, this repetition is japa. A mantra can be one syllable, many syllables or even a few sentences. When we repeat the mantra, it becomes japa. Japa should be done in the morning or during the day. Japa should not be done just before going to bed.

The spiritual heart

The spiritual heart is located right in the centre of the chest. If you find it difficult to meditate on the spiritual heart, you can concentrate on the physical heart in the chest. But after you meditate there for a few months or for a year, you will feel that inside the ordinary human heart is the divine heart, and inside the divine heart is the soul. When you feel this, you will start meditating on the spiritual heart.

Supreme

There is one God called by many different names. I like the term 'Supreme'. All religious faiths have the same God but they address Him differently. A man will be called 'Father' by one person, 'Brother' by another and 'Uncle' by another. Similarly, God is also addressed in various ways, according to one's sweetest, most affectionate feeling. Instead of using the word 'God', I use the word 'Supreme' most of the time. When we say 'Supreme', we are speaking of the Supreme Lord who not only reaches the absolute Highest, but all the time goes beyond, beyond and, transcends the Beyond.

The vital

Each human being is composed of five elements: body, vital, mind, heart and soul. There are two vitals in us: one is the dynamic vital and the other is the aggressive vital. The vital embodies either divine dynamism or hostile aggression. When the aspirant brings the soul's light to the fore, the hostile aggression changes into the divine dynamism and the divine dynamism is transformed into the all-fulfilling supreme Reality.

Emotion and the vital are two different things. You can say that the vital is the house and in that house emotion is the tenant. The most predominant emotion is the vital emotion. But emotion can also be in the body, in the mind and in the heart.